BEARING UNTOLD STORIES

Life on (and off) the Autism Spectrum

HELEN HUGHES

Book Cover by AnnMarie Reynolds for *begin a book Independent Publishers*

First paperback edition 2023

ISBN (Print) 978-1-915353-11-5
ISBN (eBook) 978-1-915353-12-2

Published by *begin a book Independent Publishers*

www.beginabook.com

For Nathan and Talia, my own reason for being and for wanting to change the world for the better.

I love you.

*"There is no greater agony
than bearing an untold story inside you "*

Maya Angelou

*"Think about what nobody has yet thought,
about that which everyone sees "*

Erwin Schrodinger

Contents

BEARING UNTOLD STORIES

Life on (and off) the Autism Spectrum

Written by

HELEN HUGHES

Published by

begin a book Writing Services & Independent Publishers

begin a book

www.beginabook.com

Chapter 1

At the beginning, and beyond Raymond Babbitt

This book as you will see, is all about stories.

The stories of people on the autism spectrum, untold until now.

This book is also about your story; but for now, we are going to start right at the beginning of our journey with autism and illustrate why we are where we are today in our understanding of neurodiversity.

I have come to realise that stories are layers, each built upon the previous one which keeps going with twists, turns and surprises around every corner. Stories are living, changing things and they never end. This is certainly true of the story of autism. I am writing this book in the summer of 2022, in a post-pandemic world and around 79 years after the first paper on autism was published.

Depending on when you read this book the story may well have changed again. It may have grown and developed even more layers, but for now let's go back to the beginning and understand why we are where we are today – both in our understanding of autism and neurodiversity as a whole.

Until fairly recently, very little was known or really understood about autism. It wasn't until the late 1970's/early 1980's that research and work on understanding autism began to gather speed.

If you were to ask someone in the street what autism is, many people will still relate their perception and comprehension of it to stereotypes.

Stereotypes that are perpetuated in the media and usually involve a geeky scientist or a tech nerd and are often male. People living through the 1980's will have been heavily influenced by the very successful movie "Rain Man". This 1988 film had huge commercial success and won a raft of awards. Starring Dustin Hoffman and Tom Cruise, Hoffman's character, Raymond Babbitt, was based on the real-life story of a man with autism, Kim Peek.

The influence of this film has meant that its portrayal of autism has remained in the public perception for the last 40 years or so. But is it accurate?

Some articles I have read suggest that the film delayed our understanding and grasp of neurodiversity (a term introduced by social scientist Judy Singer in 1998) and of maintaining the myth that people with autism are "different" to everyone else.

The narrative of 'Rain Man' could be considered to show that people with autism are disabled, complex, difficult to understand and communicate with, and that they see the world in a totally different way. The film also suggested that autistic people are brilliant with facts and figures and have an incredible memory, but lack in small talk and social skills, dictated to in no small part by their need to stick rigidly to routines. That of course is a sweeping generalisation, and one which this book will challenge.

In my job as an Occupational Therapist and Autism Specialist, I've worked with over two thousand people with autism over the last 15 years or so – as well as their families, friends, supporters and professional workers - and I have many friends on the autism spectrum. All I can say is that I have not yet met anyone like Raymond Babbitt.

Of course there are people with similar difficulties, but my point is best captured by this well-referenced quote:

"If you've met one person with autism, you've met one person with autism". (Dr Stephen Shore).

"Rain Man" did its job in showing the existence of autism as well as raising its public profile (though bear in mind that Kim Peek had a genetic condition which caused a range of problems rather than simply autism), but it didn't address the issue of individuality and the multi-dimensional spectrum of experience and being that autism really is. And it certainly didn't help us to understand and embrace neurodiversity.

Inaccurate media portrayal over the years has had an impact on the public perception of autism, which means that autistic people are still not getting the appreciation and acceptance they need and deserve.

Let's put that right.

~~~

So, what exactly is the story of autism?

To appreciate where we are today we need to take a short trip back in time and tell the story of two men who could be considered the 'fathers' of autism. Though we know that the autism journey began well before the 1920's, these two men were largely responsible for spotlighting this condition in the way we understand it today.

Leo Kanner was a Ukrainian-born doctor who moved to the United States in late 1923. He had been working as a cardiologist and GP in Germany but became interested in neurology and psychiatry and was offered the opportunity to relocate his family to South Dakota, USA so that he could take up a post at a clinic there. At that time, patients who were thought to have potential mental health conditions were often kept in institutions or 'hospitals for the feeble minded' or were offered up as domestic servants to the wealthy. They were classed as 'nature's mistakes', often sterilised against their will and asked to repeat strange phrases or count backwards in front of observing doctors. These doctors would then 'vote' on what might be wrong with these patients and prescribe strong and toxic medications which created greater psychological distress.

In those days, eugenics[1] was alive and flourishing, well before it became central to Nazi doctrines which later shocked the world. This method of 'selection' had a definite impact on how those who were "different" in any way were seen or treated. It's important to show this difficult backdrop because every story has a context. You would not be who you are without the people and places who shaped you, and your story would also be different if those elements were changed in some way. The same is true of the story of autism.

Back in the 1920's when Leo Kanner arrived in the USA, people feared difference. They were told by leaders and politicians that adults and children who spoke or moved or completed tasks in a different way were to be despised and feared. Society was educated to believe that these individuals would never amount to anything, in fact it would often be said that they should not have been born. Parents were encouraged to hide their children away in places known as "Correctional Institutions" or "Lunatic Asylums" and told to forget about their very existence.

In some of these institutions parents were encouraged to sign consent forms allowing the 'caregivers' to "shorten the child's natural life"; a legal swerve which prevented anyone from being charged with murder. The levels of neglect shown to these children though pretty much amounted to the same thing. It wasn't unheard of for the children to be starved and left outside in the snow during winter. The messaging back then was simple. If you were 'different', then you weren't wanted.

---

1 **Eugenics** - the scientifically erroneous and immoral theory of "racial improvement" and "planned breeding" - National Human Genome Research Institue

people diagnosed with autism and many countries have investigated why there has been such a marked increase. Some have looked at air quality and the fluoride levels in water whilst others have considered inoculation ingredients and processes. The reality though, is much more straightforward. We are seeing an increase in autism diagnoses because we now know its truth. That it is and can be understood as a spectrum condition.

Further, we recognise that those with autism are not 'broken', but simply see the world in a different way. Their thinking processes are not the same as those without the condition but, in the words of Erwin Lazar, the 'biggest difficulty caused by autism was that society did not understand and meet the needs of the people with it.'

Hopefully we can reflect now on how far we have come.

~~~

Compared to the days of Kanner and Asperger we are light years ahead when it comes to understanding autism but crucially, as clinicians, we don't believe this knowledge is filtering down to our larger society. Even now we find many who do not know or comprehend the story of autism and wouldn't recognise if someone were affected. If we have done so much research and our knowledge is vastly improved, how can this still be the case? Why are there still people out there who know next to nothing about this complex spectrum condition? It is my belief that there are several factors which have contributed to this:

- Clinical, health, social work and educational professionals don't get a lot of training around neurodiversity - either in their professional settings or in their careers. Given that the average GP can see anywhere up to 41 patients a day (The Times, 2018), or a teacher can typically influence 3,000 students during their career, this lack of neurodiversity training is hugely concerning. Also, we know that the best outcome is achieved with as early a diagnosis as possible so, if teachers and health professionals don't understand what autism really is, how many people can reach adulthood before anyone notices their difficulties?

A late diagnosis can cause many problems including a much higher risk of mental and physical health issues. These can be caused and exacerbated by the fact that people have had to live with this feeling of "not fitting in", or of not understanding why they have the problems they do, especially when it comes to work or relationships. Feelings of isolation and depression can lead to huge levels of stress and anxiety.

The National Autistic Society publishes data on the risk of suicide in people found to be on the spectrum which shows exponential increases year on year. The data also suggests a risk of lower life expectancy due to physical health problems. These results are hugely concerning.

- The hidden face of autism. For most people, autism isn't an outwardly observable condition (although there are some people who might show different ways of making eye contact or of walking or talking in a certain way). Often though, those on the autism spectrum look like everyone else. It is widely accepted that if others can't 'see' something, then they may not be able to understand it.

- One of the coping strategies people on the spectrum use is that of "camouflaging" or "imitating" behaviour. Broadly this means hiding who you really are and acting out a role which enables you to fit in with society. These strategies are used as protection from being singled out or bullied. One autistic young man told me it was like wearing a costume, and many people have described how tiring this is. Some of our untold stories in this book describe the impact of camouflaging and the toll it can take on somebody's mental and physical health. You will be surprised to learn that the very strategy many people with autism use to 'fit in' can actually mean they are hidden even further from society.

- Media coverage. As we've seen with "Rain Man", most of what we know and understand is due to what we are told by the media. Although there have been some improvements over recent years, on the whole neurodiversity is not something the media covers in any depth or with any great accuracy. Often, any stories that are shared have the opposite effect and can continue to perpetuate the "differences" between people. This may well have a negative outcome.

- There is still no formal way of recording how many people have autism – we don't currently have a specific register for example - we are still hypothesising how many people are actually on the spectrum. This lack of accurate data leads to estimated funding figures which means that diagnostic and support services are generally under-resourced. This leads to long waiting lists both in child and adult services throughout the United Kingdom.

- Another important factor keeping the autism story hidden is the impact of our own stories – i.e. what our brains tell us around embracing differences and dealing with the anxiety which embracing such differences may cause. I believe that we need to understand why we struggle with differences in other people and what each of us can do to overcome this, then we can all be empowered. A greater understanding can only bring positive change and the good news is, I have covered how to address your own story and thoughts in *Section Three* of this book.

~~~

In the clinical world, neurological and mental health specialities are increasing their understanding and knowledge of the massively complex human brain which means that we are constantly discovering new and exciting information through innovative research. This research includes work around why children develop autism in the first place. At present we know that it happens at an early stage of conception or development and that it is a lifelong condition, but we still don't know why some individuals are affected and others not.

If you are born with autism we know that you will die with autism, that it is a part of someone and always will be, but we still don't understand why some people develop dyspraxia or ADHD or dyslexia and why some who are on the spectrum, don't. Incidence figures vary internationally but in the United Kingdom it's estimated that autism currently affects around 1-2% of the population - that's about 700,000 men, women and children. We can't be entirely accurate though because of the aforementioned lack of robust data collection. Even if we consider those figures to be largely hypothetical that's still a lot of people affected, which just goes to show that autism is definitely not as rare as perhaps first thought.

We have also identified that autism has a significant genetic component; that is, if there is already a family member with autism, there is a higher chance of any child(ren) developing it too. Just like any other condition this is not a given, but we do know there is a higher likelihood and autism diagnosticians will usually ask a genetics-based question during an assessment.

***

To bring the story of autism to where we are right now we can summarise that:

* Autism affects every person differently.
* It can be seen as a spectrum.
* It is present at a very early stage of foetal and neuronal development.
* It can have an impact on developmental stages such as

walking and talking. Some will experience delays where others can be early walkers or talkers, and others will experience no differences at all.

* It is a lifelong condition with lifelong difficulties.
* It can run in families due to genetic significance.
* Autism affects how a person interacts and communicates with other people.
* It can impact how someone interacts with and views the world around them.
* It means that those affected have to develop different coping strategies to deal with everyday life.
* It can cause sensory or perceptual differences.
* It can have an impact on executive functioning, performance of skills and problem solving.
* Sometimes it means that people can have a Learning Disability as well, although 48-52% of autistic people are currently known to not have any intellectual difficulty or disability.
* Autism can lead to significant levels of chronic stress and anxiety throughout life.
* It can increase the likelihood of having other conditions such as ADHD (Attention Deficit Hyperactive Disorder) or Dyspraxia or Dyslexia.
* It is often misdiagnosed or overlooked, especially in older adults.
* It can cause significant mental and physical health problems, especially when someone is not diagnosed at a young age
* It can increase the risk of suicidal thoughts and actions.

In the next chapter, we will look at some of the difficulties people on the spectrum might experience and how this can affect their lives.

Chapter 2

Giving it a name

As we've seen in the previous chapter, autism is included in international diagnostic manuals such as the DSM-V (Diagnostic and Statistical Manual of Mental Disorders, Version 5) and ICD-11 (International Classification of Diseases – 11th Revision). Although these are American-based manuals, they are used across the world by clinicians.

There has been much debate though, about whether autism should be included in these manuals. Some people argue that it's a condition, a part of someone, and not a "mental disorder" or "disease". In my experience there are many people on the spectrum who feel that autism should not be seen in a medicalised way or categorised as a "disorder" but rather recognised as a difference in the way that the brain works. Whatever your viewpoint, the current inclusion in the DSM-V means that doctors and clinicians are provided with standardised guidelines, tools and structure on how to identify and diagnose autism which should mean that regardless of where you live, the clinicians you see will use a structured and standardised way of offering assessments and support.

~~~

Let's take a closer look at what it says in the DSM-V about autism. Bear in mind that the DSM-V is a medical manual which uses formal language and focuses on the negatives, i.e., the problems people have. Words such as 'deficit', 'abnormality' and 'symptoms' are regularly used so I have changed some of this formal language to make it easier to read.

It's also important to remember that the DSM is not a comprehensive reflection of autism and that there has been much criticism in the past that this manual is somewhat biased.

The DSM-5 criteria of autism consists of two main categories and then three separate requirements as follows:

Category 1: Persistent difficulties with social communication and social interaction across multiple contexts, as shown by the following (currently or in the past):

a. Problems in social-emotional reciprocity, ranging for example from abnormal social approaches and failure of normal back and forth conversation, to reduced sharing of interests, emotions or affect (mood), to a failure to initiate or respond to social interactions.

b. Problems with non-verbal communication behaviours used for social interaction, ranging from poorly integrated verbal and non-verbal communication to abnormalities in eye contact and body language, or problems in the understanding and use of gestures, to a total lack of facial expressions and non-verbal communication.

c. Problems in developing, maintaining and understanding relationships, ranging for example from difficulties adjusting behaviour to suit various social contexts, to difficulties in sharing imaginative play or in making friends, to the absence of interest in other people.

Category 2: Restricted and repetitive patterns of behaviour, interests or activities as shown by at least two of the following, currently or by history:

a. Stereotyped or repetitive motor (physical) movements, use of objects, or in speech. Such as lining up toys, flipping objects, repeating words or phrases.

a. Insisting on sameness, inflexible and needing routines or patterns of verbal or non-verbal behaviour. Such as becoming distressed at small changes, difficulties with transitions and changes, rigid thinking patterns, needing to take the same food or route every day.
b. Highly restricted or fixated interests that are intense and focused – such as strong preoccupations to unusual objects, or perseverative interests.
c. Hyperactivity (being over sensitive) or hypo reactivity (searching for stimulation) to sensory input or unusual interests in environmental sensory aspects. Examples may include apparent indifference to pain or temperature, negative responses to specific sounds or textures, excessive smelling or touching of objects, visual fascination with lights or movements.

In addition to these two categories, the person must also show:

1. That symptoms are present in the early years/development but may not become fully apparent until social demands show these limited skills, or in adults, symptoms may be hidden or masked by learned coping strategies in later life.
2. That symptoms cause significant problems in social, occupational or other important areas of current functioning
3. That the person's difficulties are not better explained by intellectual/learning disability or developmental delays. Learning disabilities and autism frequently co-occur and show that social communication will be lower than expected for the person's general development level.

Some of the difficulties an individual on the spectrum can experience might be:

* Difficulties in holding a conversation or knowing when to interject or take turns.
* Knowing what to say to other people or open a conversation.

* Taking things very literally.
* Finding it hard to make "small talk" and talking about non-specific things like the weather or what you watched on TV over the weekend.
* Knowing what to say to someone you've never met before, or with someone you're romantically interested in.
* Having difficulty coping with being in social gatherings or with lots of people, or at events like parties or weddings or celebrations.
* Knowing how to maintain a conversation, keeping it flowing without feeling awkward.
* Responding without awkwardness when someone approaches you.
* Expressing how you feel to someone else.
* Understanding the feelings of other people and reacting to these.
* Using vocal timbre, pitch and tone in a different way, such as talking too loudly or too quietly.
* Saying things that might seem blunt or inappropriate.
* (Lack of) understanding of jokes, or banter, sarcasm or metaphors.

Please remember that this is not an exhaustive list and everybody's experience will be different.

People can also struggle with non-verbal communication:

* Having problems in making or maintaining eye contact.
* Knowing what to do with your hands when you are talking.
* Using your hands to emphasise a point.
* Using facial expressions yourself or understanding what it means when other people do it.
* Using body language that's appropriate, such as not standing too close to someone or touching someone in an (in)appropriate way.

* Smiling or laughing when it's (in)appropriate.
* Understanding other people's body language, such as people turning away from you or yawning.

Autistic people can struggle with social relationships:

* Making and keeping friendships or relationships.
* Socialising with other people.
* Sharing, understanding and reciprocating emotions in relationships.
* Adjusting behaviour to suit different social circumstances or relationships.
* Sharing play or interests with other people.

Changes can be difficult for people on the spectrum to manage:

* Large transitions and changes, like moving school or starting a new job.
* Smaller changes like the house being redecorated or things being moved, or changes to someone's appearance or going on holiday.
* Needing a routine or certain ways of doing things.
* Coping when things unexpectedly change or plans fall through.

There are also other areas where autistic people might show some differences:

* Having intense or special interests in something, spending a lot of time doing it and knowing a lot about certain subjects.
* Using self-soothing or repetitive movements such as spinning or stimming.
* Being over or under sensitive to sensory experiences such as lights, sounds, smells, textures, tastes or touch.
* Struggling to recognise when you feel cold/hot or are hungry or thirsty (interoception).

* Having problems with co-ordination or with balance.
* Having differences in pain perception.
* Struggling to manage the sequence of tasks like cooking or dressing.

Remember, although it's good practice to have these guidelines for clinicians to work with, every person is an individual and their stories will all be different. Autism is a spectrum and each person will experience life and various levels of difficulty in different ways. You or someone you know might relate to *some* of these difficulties, but not necessarily all of them. Equally, individuals may have developed good coping strategies for other situations and thus these may not be problematic.

When getting a diagnosis, it is important to note that any autism spectrum difficulty must be longstanding (i.e., going back to their childhood) and will have a varying level of intensity which affects their ability to function in daily life. If, for example, you are anxious about going out and this is something you have only begun to experience recently, it will not be caused by autism. Similarly, if someone doesn't like crowds or enjoys spending time on their own, it doesn't necessarily mean they are autistic either.

We are all on a spectrum when it comes to areas such as introversion and extroversion, so it's important to recognise that not everyone who is a loner or who likes to spend time gaming or researching or enjoying Japanese Manga comic books, has autism. It's the person's whole story that is important, taken in context. The combination of things they each find difficult and the fact that these problems go back into their early years is key when it comes to considering a diagnosis of autism.

~~~

As part of a diagnostic assessment clinicians will ask for permission to speak to someone who knew that person well as a child. Ideally this will be a parent but that isn't always possible. Historical information can generally be easier to gather when assessing a child and it may have to be researched in a different way when working with adults. This might include gaining access to health records or school reports or talking to a sibling.

Of course, there are times when it's not possible to get a historical background in which case the assessment will be undertaken using observation only. That means looking at the adult person's life now, how they present in the assessment and how they are coping. Sometimes this can provide enough information for a diagnosis but clinicians will need to think of ways to work with each individual to get the information that they need. The assessment process must therefore be person-centred, empathic and consider everyone's differences.

Support should also be offered post-diagnostically which is something that we will look at in more depth in Section Four. I have also included additional information about diagnostic assessments and what to expect in the final section of this book.

A note on medication:

There is no medication for autism. Medication may be prescribed to help with issues such as anxiety or depression, but in itself there is no pharmaceutical intervention following a diagnosis of autism.

In other neurodivergent conditions interventions are different. People with ADHD can be offered medication to assist with agitation and high-energy functioning whereas those with dyslexia or dyspraxia are usually offered non-pharmaceutical interventions based on sensory or cognitive processing. Many of these solutions are provided by Occupational Therapists or specialised practitioners.

***

Due to extensive and ongoing research, autism can now be diagnosed fairly reliably from the age of around 3 years old. It is very much a social condition which impacts communication and interaction, and although there are some babies who can show differences from an early age - such as ongoing feeding or sleeping problems, a dislike of being touched or negative responses to lights or sounds – not all children will display these. Clinicians will generally need to see the child interacting and communicating with others to form a true diagnosis. By the age of 3 or 4 most children will be engaging socially in pre-school or nursery which means it's possible to observe and assess communication and social skills (generally through play) and it is here where differences can be identified.

Although we can now diagnose autism from such an early age, it is important to note that there is no upper age limit to diagnosis either. The developing story of autism means that if you were born before the late 1970's or early 1980's your chances of receiving an autism diagnosis would have been slim because we simply didn't know enough. Consequently we are now seeing 'lost' generations of older people who have struggled to either be understood or to understand their *own* differences from others and would likely have received an autism diagnosis if science had been far enough advanced. This 'lost' generation are now in their fifties, sixties, seventies and over and would be able to access a diagnostic assessment today if they so wished.

Often, in the early years of understanding autism, individuals were mis-diagnosed and I have heard many difficult and painful stories from those who were misunderstood over the years by the health care system, during their time in education or the workplace and by wider society as a whole. I have seen several patients with a diagnosis of learning disability, personality disorder or psychosis, when in fact they were actually neurodiverse. This kind of misdiagnosis can have a huge impact on that individual and those around them.

So, is a diagnosis important? Do we need to have a label?

In my own professional experience, the majority of people who have received an autism diagnosis have been positively empowered by it. Many have openly wept, relieved at finally getting answers as to why they have struggled. Others have 'self-identified' as autistic and are relieved to have this confirmed. Some though had never heard of autism and for them it became a new journey of understanding. This diagnosis enabled parents, for example, to look at their child's difficulties from a different point of view and to stop blaming themselves for their child's struggles.

The reality is that when you have:

- found it hard to communicate with other people, or have had significant anxiety from your early years;
- found it difficult to understand what the teacher was trying to say;
- not known how to make small talk with people;
- found the world to be a scary place that is harsh in its lights and sounds and smells;
- not been able to have the friendships or relationships that you really wanted;
- struggled to hold down a job or pursue the things you are interested in;
- no understanding of WHY these things are happening …

… you start to blame yourself. You turn it inwards and YOU become the failure. You believe there must be something wrong with YOU. When you think that you can't do anything right you blame YOU. You are convinced it's ALL YOUR FAULT.

When we consider these difficulties, is it any surprise that so many people experience mental health problems?

An appropriate diagnosis of autism, therefore, can reframe the understanding people have of the world.

After a diagnosis, you can learn to understand that autism has always been a part of you, that it is the outside world who doesn't 'get you' - and this realisation can be a game changer.

When a young person or adult receives a diagnosis they start to realise that many of the negative things which happened to them were NOT THEIR FAULT. This recognition can then stop the process of self-blame and when handled sensitively, move a person towards a place of empowerment and of managing the difficulties they experience on a day-to-day basis.

Getting a diagnosis can also open doors of support. A child with a diagnosis may be entitled to assistance at school, or a university student might be able to receive a grant payment for a particular piece of software or gain assistance with their coursework. An adult with a diagnosis would be legally entitled to reasonable adjustments in their workplace. All of these things can be vital in helping someone to reach their potential.

Some adults choose not to divulge their diagnosis where others like to be open about it, and there are certain occupations which require this information to be shared.

Whatever your views, a diagnosis provides understanding and acceptance. People can discover what is hard for them and find effective coping strategies. They can flourish in education, secure the job they want, get meaningful support when needed, and prevent deterioration in their mental and physical health. When you have read some of the untold stories within this book, I genuinely believe you will understand why a diagnosis of autism can be incredibly powerful.

Chapter 3

Women, Girls and Non-Binary People with Autism

I decided to dedicate a chapter of this book to the difficulties often faced by autistic females and non-binary adults. These two groups in particular can find the presentation of their autistic symptoms very different to the stereotypical assumptions and I feel it is only right to draw attention to what these differences may be. Research undertaken by Sarah Cassidy at Nottingham University in 2017 produced concerning results when looking at women affected by autism. It showed that the rates of death by suicide in those with (diagnosed and un-diagnosed) autism was highest in the middle-aged female population. A sensible conclusion was drawn that women were dying because their difficulties were being missed. Their needs were not being recognised and their voices were not being heard – but why is that exacerbated in this particular group?

Perhaps because often, we do not recognise autism in females.

~~~

Historically, more men and boys are diagnosed with autism. Current figures (2022) from the National Autistic Society show that for every three males diagnosed with autism, there is only one female diagnosed. The same ratio was seen by the NAS in 2015 when they researched the numbers of males versus females who were accessing their adult support services. This three-to-one trend has thus been consistent for at least 7 years.

There are several theories around why this male/female ratio exists;

the testosterone levels in foetuses for example, the impact of biological and environmental factors, and the fact that autistic traits are potentially unrecognised in females. There have also been suggestions that the diagnostic assessment tools have a male bias within them but fundamentally it is reasonable to argue that we simply don't understand what autism looks like in females.

So why *are* more males diagnosed with autism?

If you were to look at a primary school playground you would probably recognise the boys with autism. They are often on their own or with only one or two friends and will be separate from major large social groups. The autistic boy is unlikely to be a dominant central character and is often a target for intimidation and bullying. They may also display difficulties with verbal and non-verbal communication or they may walk or hold their bodies in a certain way. Females with autism do something else entirely.

The autistic girl learns early on in life that if you attach yourself to a social group there will be safety. They may remain on the periphery of these groups but will be far less obviously isolated than their male counterparts. Girls will also tend to adopt different coping strategies and can become adept at hiding their difficulties. Many learn that if they stay quiet, be polite, and just get on with their school work, they will avoid attracting the attention of the teacher or of the other children. This is a coping strategy which has been intuitively developed by the autistic girl to prevent them from being picked on or singled out or bullied, which is the complete opposite of the coping strategy developed by the autistic boy.

Females, many from a young age, learn the strategy of camouflaging and copying others. They will imitate the appearance or behaviour of those who they see as most socially successful and might meticulously research reality TV programmes or social media posts in an effort to learn how to be socially popular or accepted. This may not sound much different to most girls of a certain age, however females with autism will often go to extreme lengths to look or behave like their friends. As a guide, here are some behaviours that can be present in the autistic female:

* Being socially aware. They may be more socially aware than their male counterparts and/or maintain social relationships to a higher degree.
* Empathy. Many autistic females are highly sensitive and are often drawn into the "caring" professions.
* People pleasing - the need to make people like you, even when there is a cost to the person. Many females feel validated only by external praise or acceptance and may struggle to accept their own internal values.
* Social overwhelm. Spending time in school or with other people becomes exhausting, and there is a need to be alone or withdraw from others.

The fact that these behaviours can easily be present in females who *do not* have autism, shows how well the autistic female has adapted. Their 'differences' from others are not as distinct as they are in males, and this is where the problem lies.

Imagine you are a teacher in a primary school with 30 children in your class, some of whom have significant behavioural or social issues. Who would you spot first as having some difficulties?
The child who has trouble sitting still, has a loud voice and needs support to maintain their behaviour or the child who is quiet, polite and working hard?

If we believe that autism is typified by Raymond Babbitt in *'Rain Man'* or is prevalent only in male computer experts, who is going to notice it in the quiet, studious schoolgirl?

This is why so many girls and young women are not diagnosed during their educational years. By the time these girls leave school it is entirely possible they will have been through a host of negative experiences, with no identifying cause being investigated or found. These experiences can easily lead to social, personal and emotional distress for the girl which sadly increases their suicide risk.

We know from research that recognising autism early is the key to ensuring successful life outcomes and if we are not recognising the signs how can we possibly reach an early diagnosis? Every adult who today presents for an autism assessment is a child who fell through the net – and this is particularly prevalent in women and girls. Some of the untold stories in this book demonstrate the difficulties faced by females on the spectrum and it is my hope that by telling these stories, understanding can grow throughout our communities so that we can pick up those early warning signs. Reading these stories and listening to the voices of those affected can have a profound effect, not least on our ability to prevent further distress, trauma and ultimately – needless deaths.

Section 2

Bearing Untold Stories

Introduction

As a little girl, for some unknown reason, I wanted to be a train driver. Actually, I really wanted to be a nurse but I hated the sight of blood so the natural alternative was to drive fast trains through tunnels – I still can't really work out how those two occupations are connected!

Regardless of my childhood motivations however, what I ended up becoming was an Occupational Therapist. I really believed in and wanted to embrace the idea of empowering people, of helping them to reach their full potential despite setbacks of illness or disability or often just circumstance, and so it became a natural choice to choose Occupational Therapy as my eventual career.

After graduating from university I joined the NHS in 1992 and have worked for our national health service ever since. Most of my time has been in mental health services - on hospital wards and in community teams - and although I spent many years working hard to lead teams and shape services, it was with my patients that I always felt the greatest sense of meaning.

In 2011, as part of a routine visit, I went to see a young man at home who had been referred to the mental health service with depression. When I got to his flat I sensed something different about him. Ian (not his real name) was sitting in total darkness wearing sunglasses and was surrounded by a collection of decorative soldiers - all set up in ranks on every surface around the room. He showed me each battalion, each rank, and told me about their victories and defeats in various wars. Ian talked to me but he never once looked at me. Every now and again he would rhythmically rock his body and I could sense there was some anxiety about me being in his flat.

Ian told me he had a diagnosis of autism, which at the time was something I knew little about despite my extensive training and clinical experience. So, I did some research. I went away and read up on autism and, with Ian's help, we started to navigate some difficult waters together. My goal was to resolve some of the social problems that Ian had in his life at that time but after each visit I came away feeling uneasy. The world of health care is complex and there were many conditions I knew very little about. Despite my recent learnings I still realised I had barely scratched the surface of understanding autism. Anxiety, depression, bipolar disorder, schizophrenia – these I worked with on a daily basis but autism, that was still a mystery.

Often coincidental events align and a few months after first meeting Ian I was offered a secondment. It was at a new service that was being established with local funding. The project? An autism support team which would assess adults for referral and if they received a diagnosis, provide support thereafter. I thought of Ian and it was a no-brainer.

My autism story had begun.

~~~

Since then I have met many people with autism. I have also met their families, supporters and carers. I have cried with a 70-year-old woman as she finally got her diagnosis. Why had people been so demeaning and abusive to her? Now at least some of her life made sense. I have held the hand of an 18-year-old young woman who had a suicide plan for the very next day simply because she didn't 'fit in'. I have looked into so many pairs of eyes and told them "This is not your fault. You are not broken". I have reassured mothers who feel the pain of guilt because they didn't "see it sooner". And I have seen the changes which happen when people realise they no longer have to hide away. I have watched them go to university, fall in love and recover mentally and physically from years of despair.

A diagnosis of autism is not a magic wand but it does hold the power of meaning and understanding, of putting things into their rightful context and of seeing yours or your loved one's autism story for the truth it really is.

As I continued on my own autism journey I began to open my thinking wider. I thought about 'difference', about what it meant and if we really are all so different. As a clinician and a human being, how different am I from the people I have worked with? Don't we all want the same things, like love, understanding, belonging, hope, health and joy?

These thoughts led me to a profound realisation: In order to understand people who think differently, we have to look at our own selves. We have to look at how we have built and developed our communities and how we chose who is "normal" or accepted and who isn't. We should consider how we have built pyramids of meaning around identity, significance and status. All of our social rules and beliefs have been created by the stories of individual people - people who went on to become influential and to establish services such as our schools, health systems and work places. In fact, we also need to acknowledge that other decisions were also made along the way which have affected our understanding too. 'Someone' decided that women should not vote, for example, and 'someone else' decided that our working hours should be 9am – 5pm Monday to Friday. These are decisions that were made and accepted by us without any real conscious consideration and one of these decisions centred around autism. Someone decided that people who have autism are disabled – and we are perhaps guilty of buying into that too.

Through my research I now know that people with autism have never been broken or different or disabled, it was all a story - about the world in which we live.

Drs Asperger and Kanner showed us that people with autism were, and still are to some extent, living in a world where they were hidden away because of a societal inability to understand and accept their differences, and this is not okay. Now, today, with the reading of this book and its untold stories, this changes.

All of the stories are from people I have met and walked with – if only for a time in their journey. I have been privileged to be a part of their stories but that did not detract from the sadness I felt when I realised these would remain untold, unnoticed by a world still struggling to understand. That's when I knew I had to bring them to life. That I had to recount these to anyone who would read and listen so that wider society could change but not only that, so that those hiding their stories would no longer be alone.

As I said, with this book, these stories, now it changes. Whether you are on the spectrum or not, it's time to see those with autism and associated challenges for who they are, not for who we think them to be.

Read on. Listen. Hear.

And step into your light.

The Untold Stories

I have categorised these stories into themes and although they largely speak for themselves I have added an introduction and some comments to put them into context. You will also find a Glossary at the end of this section to define words or phrases which may be unfamiliar. Words or phrases which appear in the Glossary are denoted by **_bold italic font_**.

And a note of caution: these stories are the authentic and honest accounts of real people written in their own words from their perspective and apart from some basic editing, they have not been changed. With this in mind, you may find some of the stories tough to read.

Theme One: Camouflaging and Coping

The Skins I Weave by Rebecca

Rebecca was diagnosed with autism at the age of 22. Her story outlines how hard it can be to consciously learn social rules that other people might have picked up without thinking - like understanding facial expressions, making small talk with unfamiliar people and recognising the nuances of non-verbal communication such as smiling. Her story also shows us how creating an identity as a woman with autism can be challenging; many girls and women use camouflaging strategies to try and fit in whilst hiding who they really are. The burden of this causes significant mental health pressures, and for many people like Rebecca, leads to self-harm and depression.

When I was around eight years old in the mid-1990's my class in school had a talk from a mental health specialist. They sat us down in a semi-circle and explained that some people have difficulty knowing what to say, how to say it, and in understanding what other people are feeling. It was the job of these specialists apparently to teach children with this problem how to communicate properly. They then brought out a large piece of paper with lots of drawings of faces on it and asked the class which face represented which feeling. They pointed to one in the middle - a big round red face with an upturned mouth and steam coming out of its head.

"Angry!" said one of my classmates. I frowned in confusion.

"Very good!" said the specialist.

"Wait."

My hand shot up in the air, and the specialist looked at me in surprise.

"Yes?" she asked.

"That's not what people look like when they're angry."

Some of my classmates began to titter quietly.

"What do you mean?" she asked, patiently.

"Well," I said, "their face doesn't go red. And smoke doesn't come out of their head. The frown and the eyebrows are right, but what about when people are angry, but their faces don't show it? Like when Mrs Duncan wants us to be quiet and is trying not to shout?"

There was a definite murmur of quiet laughter surrounding me now. I heard a boy near me whispering about how stupid I was.

"Calm down, calm down," said our teacher, sitting with her arms folded in the corner.

"Those are some good questions. And of course, people's heads don't really start smoking. This is just an example," the specialist explained slowly, as the laughter died down.

I frowned in confusion, "Well the example doesn't make sense then."

"This is just one example," replied the specialist exasperatedly, "maybe when you see the others it will start to make sense".

And with that, she moved onto the other faces on the paper, and I sat in quiet confusion until she brought out another sheet.

"Now these are examples of normal conversations that people have with each other. The first one starts: 'The weather is bad today'. What sort of things would you say back to that?"

I frowned. 'The weather is bad today' isn't a question - surely it didn't need a response? Also, who actually talks about the weather?

"Yes, it is. It's been raining a lot." A shy girl piped up next to me.

"Very good," said the specialist, "can you think of anything else to say in a conversation?"

The boy who'd called me stupid put his hand up in the air. "How about 'What did you watch on TV last night?'"

I tried not to laugh. That seemed like such a silly question when there are so many more interesting things to talk about.

"Great!" said the specialist, "Anything else?"

The specialist began writing the questions down on the whiteboard. Once she had five she grouped us up and got us to try asking and answering them.

"These examples are a bit stupid, aren't they?" I asked the girl I'd been paired with quietly, "I mean, 'What's your favourite colour?' - really? Do they think we're babies?"

"My favourite colour is purple" she responded tiredly. "Can you just ask me and get on with the questions? It's break time soon."

~~~

It is worth noting that the mainstream school I went to was not, as is colloquially known, any sort of "Special Educational School". What I later learned was that there were some boys in the class who had been diagnosed with 'social problems' and the specialists coming into class was a way of the school giving those boys some help with communication skills without unfairly singling them out. It is also worth noting here that I wasn't diagnosed with autism until I was in my early twenties. Hard to believe, in retrospect.

I later learned that many of the 'conversation starters' given in that social skills session were not, in fact, patronising clichés, but indeed genuinely used by my peers well into adulthood. The pictures of facial expressions were much less useful.

On my first day of high school, I made eye contact with a girl sitting near me. She continued to stare until the break bell rang before then declaring me her enemy. She snapped every time I talked to her, much to my confusion. It is only when I recently looked back at the imprinted image of her face in my mind that I realised she was actually smiling at me in that first lesson and trying to get me to smile back. She must have thought I was incredibly rude when I didn't.

~~~

In 2008, when I was 15 years old, I was part of a teen depression therapy group because of the mental health problems I was having. No one - not even I - knew that I was autistic at that point. So even in a group of 'weird' kids, I was the weird kid.

It's safe to say that I was not very good at the group therapy thing but being around people my own age who had gone through similar problems and listening to their stories made me feel much less isolated. After about a year of group therapy I wasn't getting any better. The depression, self-harm and suicidal ideation was as present as my first day there, and someone, somewhere in the system, decided that there was no point in inviting me to come to therapy again.

My mother broke the news gently by telling me that an hour of therapy every week was distracting me from my studies too much - so a benevolent, eponymous *'they'* had decided I needn't return. Retrospectively I feel like the constant thoughts of suicide and regular self-harming was far more distracting than one hour of therapy a week, and removing me from the group only served to increase my feelings of rejection and isolation, but at the time I was so overwhelmingly dead inside that those emotions were nothing more than grains of sand in the ocean of desert I was drowning in.

~~~

Safe to say that my exams did not go well but the end of them meant I could finally transition back into my therapy group. At the meeting to discuss readmission, the head of some vaguely titled psychology department was there with the therapist I had been working with over the past year. He sat with his arms folded while my mother explained to my old therapist that I felt like I needed to return. After she had finished he peered down to me over his glasses and asked, "Are you sure you feel it is necessary to come back?"

"Yes," I replied, and I can recall even now, exactly how hollow my torso felt.

"No one in the group now are the same people who were in it before, when you were there," he said.

"Okay," I responded, unsure of his point.

"What I mean is," he continued, "if you're looking just to socialise then you may not fit into this new group."

My ex-therapist looked uncomfortable. "I'm sure Rebecca would get along."

"Why did the old group stop coming?" I asked, finding it odd that they should all be gone after only a few months.

"After you left," my ex-therapist said delicately, "members of the old group started trickling out."

I felt a sharp stab of guilt in my gut. Had my leaving somehow inspired the others to quit doing the therapy they desperately needed?

"How did your exams go?" the man asked, looking at the wall clock.

"Fine," I lied.

"And the coping mechanisms from the Cognitive Behavioural Therapy you were given helped you?" he asked.

"Sure," I lied again, despite the fact that CBT never actually worked for me, not wanting to insult the therapist.

"So, you're seeing improvements?" he asked nonchalantly.

I was quiet for a moment.

"Rebecca?" My mum prodded me.

"Mm-hm." I hummed quietly.

"Well in that case," he said in a tone of strained positivity, "it might be nice to have you back. Just for one session, mind."

"Why just one session?" I asked.

"So you can talk about how much better you are! You're one of the old group of patients who successfully got over their problems. It'll be really encouraging for our new group to see what they could become."

What they could become.

I was too stunned to say no.

~~~

The day came for my grand appearance.

I put on my makeup, did my hair and wore a new dress that my dad had bought me to try and cheer me up. It hadn't worked, but I appreciated the gesture all the same.

My hair was a tight short black crop. A new style that I had cut myself after I'd had a breakdown only a short while before. I wanted to become a different person. I wanted to cut away parts of myself. To be reborn. The dress was sleeveless, and in a moment of proud defiance I chose not to wear a cardigan over it. I wanted the fresh cuts on my arms to be seen. My anger at the injustice of the situation was limp, but present. I remember sitting in a circle with this new group of faces staring at me. I remember being introduced by my ex-therapist who was smiling.

59

I replicated her smile mindlessly; something I had never done before, as smiling without merit or need exhausted and confused me.

But that day I smiled. And the room smiled back.

"Rebecca is doing much better now, aren't you Rebecca?" she asked me.

"Yep." I said, smiling a smiley smile.

I don't remember much of what was said in the therapy session but I can still see the faces of the people in it. I can see how kind and happy they were, how encouraged they felt at the sight of me.

And I remember whilst I was sitting there, that I had a revelation which changed my life for both the better, and worse, forever.

I can pretend, I thought.

I can pretend and no one will notice.

I can pretend and make people happy.

I can pretend and people will be nice to me.

I can pretend.

I can pretend.

I can pretend.

~~~

So was born my first mask, and it was a simple one. Just a smile and a positive attitude. I was surprised at how authentic it was. I was surprised no -one called me out on it.

Maybe people saw the truth and looked past it.

Maybe no one cares if you're lying - as long as the lie makes them happy.

~~~

At the end of the therapy session, everyone was handed a piece of paper and told to write our name at the top. We were to pass them around the circle and everyone was to write something positive about the individual who owned the paper.

It was easy writing positive things about everyone else as they had all been so overwhelmingly kind and welcoming to me, a kindness which I felt I did not deserve. It was reading my own paper which was painful. I still own it but I haven't looked at it in a long time. It read things like:

'It was great to meet you!'
'You're so cool and I love your hair'
'That dress is so pretty and you are so honest and open'

And the real nail in the coffin:

'I'm proud of you for getting better. I hope I can get better someday.'

On the drive home I sat slumped in the passenger seat. My insides were a swirling galaxy of guilt and pain and sadness. I had never felt less proud of myself, and that's saying something. But I had learned something about myself that day. Something shameful yet useful. I had learned that I could pretend. So what is a human meant to be?

It is a question constantly redefined by fashion or religion or politics. And depending on the person who is answering, the response varies hugely, with the most common one simply being 'themselves' with the unspoken caveat that whoever 'they' are must meet these unspoken definitions.

Humanity's social evolution involves the subconscious recognition of human traits in others. The specific traits that quantify humanity are influenced by cultural values, but they are always there. But what if you're born without the ability to subconsciously recognise or absorb these traits? What if you need to be taught something that no one consciously learns?

There is no 'Behaving Normally for Dummies' so the only way to learn is to observe and practice. So, after this first experience of masking, I began to observe and I practiced. And as I did that I formed my masks, working on a craft, inserting small changes.

A smile or sympathetic look here, a reassuring phrase there.

Eye contact, no, not *that* much eye contact, *that* much eye contact.

Sit like this, don't do that with your hands.

That's an inappropriate subject, but somehow this isn't?

Even if the behaviours I was mimicking didn't make sense I sewed them into the fabric anyway and embroidered new faces for myself, different ones for different situations, places and people. Just like everyone else does, I suppose.

The only difference being that I put my masks on with purpose and intention – not to manipulate, but to hide and survive.

~~~

I imagine that the acknowledgement of feigning human traits suggests that I do not have the emotional capabilities that would ordinarily fuel them, but that is simply untrue. It's not that I don't feel, it's that I don't show what I'm feeling in the same way everyone else does, which is particularly complicated when you're a woman.

Masking is widely known to be more common in women, and this is often treated in a congratulatory manner, deemed a result of an inherent difference between the psychology of women and men. On the contrary, my personal observations have shown that this difference is sociological rather than psychological.

Women are told every day who they are meant to be down to the finest detail, to an extent where men I've known have expressed disbelief at the extremity of this control when I've described it to them. These standards are levied upon women before we even open our mouths. Women are haunted by the expectations of predetermination.

What is she wearing?
Does she have anyone with her?
What are they wearing?
How does she sit, stand, talk?
A man sat alone is a man sat alone.
A woman sat alone is a bitch who can't get along with others.

All this leads to autistic women being better at masking because they have a very specific constricted template to live by which is handed to them practically from birth, as with any woman.

It is nothing to be either proud or ashamed of.

It is something to be angry about.

~~~

I don't think that there's a place where people, autistic or not, mask more than the workplace. Only now your head is doubly weighed down by the mask of not just 'normal human' but 'professional normal human'. And don't get me started on the multi-layered cluster of masks involved in 'fun' work outings. But when the way you present yourself is key to your financial stability, the pressure can become unbearable.

Passing a job interview is hard enough for someone with socio-normative behavioural patterns, which is why becoming employed can be near impossible for members of the autistic community.

So, when I somehow managed to successfully finish university and gain employment, it's safe to say I was both shocked and overly eager to cling to whatever job was offered to me, even to the detriment of myself. Desperate to please, but with no knowledge as to how, and constantly feeling unsure of the boundaries of my verbal and non-verbal communications combined with standard work-related concerns, meant that for at least eight hours a day, 5 days a week, I was an overwhelmed, confused, mess of anxiety.

My mental health devolved to the point where I needed to cover up the pain in my mind with a new pain - a more controllable pain. Hunger was the easiest to attain; just don't eat, or purge what you do. Then it became physical. The works bathroom was a great escape. I began by scratching the sharp corner of my work key card over my stomach. In my head I would imagine it cutting deep and my guts spilling out on the ground and into the toilet bowl for everyone to see. This escalated to the development of my 'work survival toolbox': an old pencil case with a pair of sharp sewing scissors, antibacterial wipes and plasters inside. I took this with me to the bathroom and made use of it in the four plastic walls of semi-privacy a cubicle brings.

From then on, short sleeves and bare legs were no longer an option.

Which brings me to the following question: Why are all office clothes so itchy, tight and downright painful to wear?

I have what is known as heightened sensory perception, meaning that the everyday discomfort which non-autistic people may be able to push to the back of their mind is instead right at the forefront. That suit, which may be a little uncomfortable to you, is sandpaper on my skin. Adding physical pain to the emotional one I was trapped in, plus the pressure of having to hide it all and find excuses for any elements of my true self that slipped out, all led me to an experience held by many autistic individuals: an autistic burnout.

When a computer is overworked, overheating and overburdened by too many systems being open at any one time, it protects itself by shutting itself down into a safe mode. In this mode the computer returns to its most basic usage, but in order to return to functioning to its full potential, it needs to be repaired. Just like when I experience an autistic burnout.

And what happens if you can't stop? If the computer is forced to reboot again and again without being repaired?

It crashes, over and over, until its key components are rendered unusable. That was when I simply stopped going into work. That was when I stopped being able to speak, or think, or move. The layers and layers of mask weighed down my face until my nose was dragging against the ground. The fabric I had weaved was torn away, and the face underneath came with it.

That was when I was diagnosed.

~~~

It was hard, at first, to even reach the point where I could tell someone how I felt with any accuracy. After so many years of meticulously hiding everything, all of a sudden I had to reveal it to a stranger with a clipboard.

Creating a mask is about hiding the things that you are not, but the process of peeling them away is about showing the things that you are. Difficult, when you've been told your whole life that who you are is wrong.

I was incredibly lucky to be put in the hands of Helen for this process, to whom I owe a great debt of gratitude. I have a face, and a life to live and wear it, because of her.

After my diagnosis I was exposed to a new challenge: peeling away the layers of mask. Readying myself for the fallout of rejections and insults and statistically lower employment rates. I knew what I was getting myself into, but it was hard not to care.

'Still,' I thought, 'it would be nice to let my skin breathe for once.' And perhaps I would be alone, but at least I would be myself.

But in the process I found that I also began to peel away my own skin and expose the flesh and muscle and veins underneath. I wanted to prove to myself that a human being existed under that layer of skin. Wearing a mask all the time makes you forget even yourself. It is a form of self-destruction. It keeps you safe and miserable.

I do still sometimes put one on for specific occasions as everyone does, autistic or otherwise. But now I can take them on and off with purpose over my raw, re-developing face.

And as re-growing that face is a task I am still undergoing, I find that, against my own predictions, I am not doing it alone. With every strong new layer of dermis my group of family and friends grows stronger too. And, furthermore, I now have the frankly incredible assurance that they are here to see my own skin, not ones I've weaved.

~~~

George Bernard Shaw once described England and America as two countries separated by a common language. But when Mr Shaw said that it was 1942 and the Wi-Fi wasn't as good. Due to the rise of the internet a linguistic bridge has been built between these two nations via shared media sources, resulting in this historic language barrier gradually being broken down. People from these two countries can now peek over the metaphorical bricks and communicate, not by necessarily adopting the other's language, but by recognising the Americanisation's or Briticisms that the other uses.

It seems to me that autistic and non-autistic people are also separated by a common language, although this language is not verbal. It is the language of the subconscious, the facial expressions and vocal variations and body language subtleties that are adopted by everyone, autistic or not. The only differences between these forms of non-verbal communication are that the non-autistic version is deemed socially appropriate.

For example, a commonly acceptable way of expressing happiness is to smile.

Whereas a common (although not universal) way for autistic people to express happiness is to flap our hands. I personally do this a lot, and frankly, I often do not realise it is happening unless people point it out to me. Hence my way of communicating is just as subconscious as a smile. But now you know this about me I am sure that if we ever meet you will recognise my hand-flapping as a sign of happiness, and hopefully smile, or flap, in turn.

'But' I hear you ask internally, 'if the form of communication is subconscious, then how can we extrapolate and define the meaning of each communicative pathway and provide translations of them to the other party? Who could possibly complete such a task?' And my response will be another question: 'Have you not read the above chapter?'

There is no one more qualified to translate the intricacies of human behaviour than one who has been forced to learn it through necessity. The spectator sees more of the game, after all.

Of course, it would be easy to say that learning each other's languages is highlighting rather than eliminating our differences, and we all simply need to accept each other for who we are. But when has humanity ever been good at that? This concept completely dismisses our evolutionary instinct to distrust and protect ourselves from the unrecognisable.

Sometimes I wonder if, when I remove my mask and communicate with strangers in a way that seems natural to me, they experience the uncanny valley effect. Like, 'It looks like a human and it sounds like a human, but there is something not quite human here. Or at least, not what I recognise as humanhood.' Therefore, the 'Peace, Love and Acceptance, dude', attitude does no one any favours. It dismisses an aspect of human nature which cannot be erased and attempts to enforce an ideal which very few people will accept. It's a philosophical argument, not an actionable solution.

The only way to place everyone on equal footing is to learn how to recognise humanity in all its forms, not only as the ideal. And frankly, autistic people have already done a hell of a lot of footwork in this area.

It's about time everyone else started to recognise the humanity in us.

~~~***~~~

Daydreaming *by Bran*

Bran is a university student diagnosed with autism in her mid-twenties. Her story raises the issues of sensory differences which people on the spectrum often experience along with the exhaustion of trying to predict a complex world, the challenges of our education systems and having a co-diagnosis of Attention Deficit Hyperactivity Disorder (ADHD).

My story with **neurodivergence** is like many others except I did not realise I was living it. I had no real idea of the story I found myself embroiled in until I was in my mid-twenties.

For over two decades I had felt out of place and 'off' compared to those around me. This jarring feeling was something I'd just come to live with - you develop ways of coping and strategizing the world around you, an expert at navigating uncertain waters - your very own master mariner. The experience of doing so without understanding yourself though is a tiring one - to explore the world with extra difficulty, having to exert energy into the gruelling trial and error of social situations, education, work, and all myriad of everyday tasks. All often without understanding why it seems to take you so much more mental and physical effort compared to your peers. It's like running an invisible marathon and more so, it's lonely.

It never occurred to me that the buzzing sensation and nausea I experienced when seeing car taillights at night was not something everyone could relate to, or that cardboard and the touch of paper is something that sent a repulsed shiver down only my spine yet others seemed not to mind this insidious texture. Other people either were not expressing it, or perhaps I was to blame?

Maybe I was too weak?

Too sensitive to the world around me?

Either way, others seemed to have little to no outward struggle with the everyday, or at least not the same parts of the everyday that I did. As a sort of balance though, neither did they benefit from my unique quirks; their sense of smell and taste seemed quite separate, whereas I was able to experience an intertwined depth of taste infused with smell - something I later came to learn is **synaesthesia**. Others were restricted to a more linear indulgence.

Likewise, my sense of hearing and direction at times have confused my peers. From early childhood I have been viewed almost suspiciously for my inert ability to find my way in unfamiliar places without need for maps or direction - something that came in very handy later in life when wandering around mega-cities on the other side of the earth.

Somewhat harder to find the words to explain, especially in my high school days, was that I could work far easier in a dark room than one bathed in light - sounds counter intuitive right? Most teachers logically jumped to the conclusion that I was being deliberately awkward or I had some form of photosensitivity.

Neither was the case but at the time I was lacking the necessary words to properly explain that the squealing high pitch vibrations of the electrical current pulsing through the walls were palpable and distressing to me and made it impossible for me to concentrate.

So, I was labelled the disruptive or lazy kid, one that cared little for learning and would simply sit daydreaming into oblivion. Once the system decides you fit into a box it seems there is no real getting out of it. I tumbled through the school system, chronically underachieving, despite often being described as bright - an all-too-common experience for neuro-divergent people it seems.

Secondary education wasn't a particularly positive environment - state schools in the early 2000's simply didn't have the time or resources to properly cater to the needs of anyone who was outside of the conventional norm. I dropped out of education entirely by the age of 15, the levels of stress and discomfort brought about by puberty coupled with a turbulent home life simply left no mental energy for participating in a hostile school environment. I sat my GCSE's more out of boredom than real desire.

Needless to say, I once again underachieved - not one result at C or above. To many this only solidified their belief that "I wouldn't amount to much" as one particular teacher put it.

Neurodivergent people might seem as if we have our heads in the clouds 99% of the time but be very careful what you say because if I do catch what you are saying, I tend to have a very long and accurate memory.

Words stick with me. For a long time.

~~~

As the years went by, and on the insistence of well-meaning family members, I started and dropped out of numerous further education and college courses. Again people assumed I was lazy or obstinate in my desire to waste away my teenage years sitting indoors playing video games. This was not the case of course, I just had not yet found the right motivation to want to achieve these things.

The first step towards higher education for me came from an unlikely and ironic source - video games. I used to play an online interactive game in which players would create characters, quest together and act out adventures via text. This became a hyper fixation for me. The idea that I could collaboratively create a rich and detailed story with others was almost intoxicating. I HAD to do it!

I tried - I made my character and jumped in but I was told that people couldn't understand me. I had left high school with shockingly poor English and undiagnosed dyslexia which effectively barred me from taking part. I was semi-literate at best and was faced with being denied the opportunity to share my creativity.

So, I learned. I threw myself at the challenge and, over the course of a year, I had developed my English capability to the point that not only was I able to role-play online, but I was now also writing essays for the night school English course I had enrolled on at the local college.

This was the beginning. From here my sights started to wander and widen. If I could do this on my own what else could I do?

~~~

University had always been something that other people did; it was a middle-class fantasy that people like me simply did not have an investment in. Though now I could not help but daydream - what if I wanted that experience too? Against the warnings and concerns of my family I successfully applied for and secured a place at a prestigious university.

It had taken me five years longer than my peers to get to the higher education stage of my life, but I did get there - on my own terms and without GCSE results. Though it was undoubtedly harder I still got there.

There is a stigma surrounding the 'space cadet'- the neuro-divergent person whose head is constantly in the clouds - but without the ability for daydreaming, I honestly doubt I would ever have been able to achieve anything. If I have one superpower in my arsenal it is the ability to daydream – and to daydream fiercely! Coupled with this, it seems to me that if there is one thing that motivates neuro-divergent people more than anything else it is indignation. Treat us poorly or criticise us too harshly and we might leave you with egg on your face!

~~~

University was tough, the exponential learning curve was immense and I very quickly began to fall behind. Being a first-generation scholar I had no support network to rely on and the experience was intense. I may have been over 21 when I started my degree, but I was certainly not an adult until the end of it.

During my first year I was taken aside by a tutor who asked me if I might have **dyslexia** and subsequently referred me for an assessment. This was the first time in my 22 years of education that someone had noticed I was struggling.

I was assessed and not only was I confirmed as dyslexic but also **dyspraxic**. This assessment led to others and suddenly my world was filled with words and acronyms such as **Autism, ASD, ADHD, Fibromyalgia** and **PTSD**.

I was struggling to make sense of this newfound recognition of self, waiting to be seen by specialists whilst not only trying to navigate the stress of academia but also handling the fall-out of an incredibly unhealthy and abusive relationship in which I was involved at the time.

My life was thrown into turmoil after I found the courage to leave my abusive ex. For the next two years I had to take time off from studying whilst dealing with unfound accusations, the police and the stress and uncertainty that the situation brought.

I finally received my autism diagnosis which, for the first time in my life, enabled me to access pro-active support to help me understand the way that my brain works. It was a tricky time, equally distressing and revelatory.

Getting to know yourself deeply can be emotionally draining, unlearning years of internalised shame for simply existing and being different is a hard, hard journey. I was able to get support to live independently for the first time and I learnt ways of coping with sensory stress as well as rebuilding my self-confidence and trust in people. With much support from the Autism Diagnostic Team and meeting others on the spectrum I learned a great deal in the two years that I took out of academia, and I was so much better for it.

~~~

When I was in a position to return to my degree, I did so from a place of empowerment. I put the negative experiences of my first attempt behind me and threw myself into the first year of my degree. I made a multitude of friends and embraced many new and often daunting opportunities that came my way. I joined at least half a dozen student societies and became involved in my university disability association and student welfare teams. I went from being an anxious wreck to a student who cared deeply for the wellbeing of my peers, and worked to fix some of the institutional failings of my university.

I passed my first year with a high grade. More importantly though, I got to be a student and achieve my potential. I was able to live an experience that I had always been told was off limits to people like me, and I will never forget it.

During my second year I was doing well but there were still a few things that did not quite line up with my autism diagnosis. It was suggested to me that perhaps some of my issues around **sensory processing**, time management, impulsivity and intrusive thoughts might better be understood through the lens of ADHD.

At first this seemed odd to me; in my mind ADHD was specifically a condition characterised by excessive energy and hyperactive tendencies, something that many who know me would not necessarily attribute to me. I soon came to learn however, that far from my preconceptions,

ADHD is a complex mesh of different symptoms which can include the former but also much, much more.

It was through the YouTube videos of **Jessica McCabe** that I realised this made a whole lot of sense. I most likely have been dealing with ADHD symptoms and the difficulties it can cause my entire life. It is no easy feat trying to navigate a society that is not only woefully designed to be ADHD friendly but often stigmatizes people with non-neurotypical experiences. Again, I underwent an assessment process and of little surprise was another positive diagnosis.

The first line of treatment for ADHD is stimulant medication, which although it sounds counterintuitive, tends to give clarity, and at least in my case slows my brain down so that I can reach an operable level. The therapeutic element of treatment for me was very similar to that which I had undergone immediately following my autism diagnosis. The medication was the final piece of the brain puzzle.

~~~

Equipped with both the strategies I had learned over the previous few years and now the medication which allowed me to find a consistent baseline, I was well prepared to achieve the best I possibly could.

I aced my second year. I managed to establish a great social circle, my academic work was in the top 5% of my class and I even managed to find the time to volunteer and attend academic conferences around the country. I also proudly came out as LGBTQ (see glossary), something I had not felt at all confident in doing just a few years earlier.

My life began to take shape.

~~~

I was happy, but I could not escape the feeling of being saddened that I had been forced to waste so many years before reaching this point. If I had achieved so much in the space of a year, imagine what I could have done with the ten years between leaving high school and then?

Apparently I am not alone in this - many people have a similar reaction. First comes the euphoric excitement that you are no longer held back, struggling to understand why you find everyday tasks more taxing than you should, often lacking the language to adequately describe the experience. After the awe at this new-found potential comes the inevitable feeling of loss - loss for all that time spent silently contending with this unknown dilemma.

I lacked the comfort of having too long to dwell on this as, immediately after my second year of study, I took part in an international field trip to Rome, and three days after that I travelled 5,700 miles to Japan. Not being able to speak a word of the language didn't stop me. That's a pretty big achievement for the kid who at one point was far too nervous to take public transport and much too afraid to go to the shops because she was crippled with social anxiety.

The very same person who was once paralysed with fear over answering the phone, now found herself navigating Tokyo in rush hour and climbing mountains on the far side of the globe.

I do not think I ever really imagined I was capable of that. It would not have come to reality had I not been allowed time to hyper-fixate on video games and teach myself how to write. This was not the achievement of the education system; it was my achievement.

~~~

The final year of my degree was going so, so well. That is until it was not.

My grades were better than ever, I was powering through with my eyes set on postgraduate level study and I even managed to visit the USA and see the sights of Washington D.C. - my fourth continent out of seven! The year ahead was set to be a triumphant bang with which to herald in the next decade, but this was not to be an ordinary year.

It was 2020, the year the world in a very tangible way came to a halt. The experiences of millions of people are testament to the hellish nature of the first year of the new decade. The nuance with which 2020 was painful for many is palpable, but the total collapse of routine and progression for neuro-divergent people was particularly difficult. In the span of the previous two years I had achieved the highest grades of my academic career, canvassed to be a representative for my student union and even entered new romantic relationships. In the turbulent wash that 2020 became I contracted Covid-19, had to drop out of canvassing and my relationship, like many people's, became rocky and ultimately unsustainable. I became homeless for a period and suffered significant bereavement.

My academic progression was drop-kicked, floored even, by all of this. I had to take time away from study again. I did not get to graduate alongside my peers and the shame that this left me feeling hit incredibly hard.

Despite all my achievements I still felt less than - perhaps my teachers, family and naysayers had been right all along?

In truth it was not until coming to write this explanation of my journey that I realised how little it actually matters. It has been a rough year, an awful year and yes it has set me back, but I am so much bigger than my difficulties, so much more as a person than the labels or even struggles presented by autism or ADHD. I have not failed. I am just taking the long way around. The end of my degree is within sight, it is attainable and in taking that less clear path I am stopping to smell the flowers and go on adventures.

I am so much better-rounded as a person, and I have so many more stories to tell.

This is the lesson in my story:

Do not follow your dreams, chase them. Even if it feels impossible, and it may well be, you will not know where you will end up until you start. It does not have to be a sprint or a gruelling marathon - a steady walk will do. One foot in front of the other. Just keep moving and see where it takes you, down untrodden paths and un-navigated waters.
Don't ever give up hope.

Take on the criticism of others but use it to your advantage. And don't ever stop daydreaming. It is your very own superpower and who knows where it will lead you.

You may not be on the autism spectrum yourself but there are things you can do that will make life better for you too. Listen and support neurodivergent people irrespective of whether you understand our experience or trajectory through life. When we are ready - trust me - we are likely to jump in feet first and with unrivalled tenacity and there will be no stopping us.

Use caution when making assumptions about people and deciding what a neuro-divergent person is capable of, ascribing their value or limiting them based upon what you deem they are fit to achieve. You might well seed a steel-clad determination in us to spend a lifetime proving you wrong. A long time ago someone told me I would not succeed.

So, I did.

~~~***~~~

Note: Bran has achieved a First Class Honours in her degree since writing this story.

Stephanie Versus Shoelaces *by Stephanie*

Stephanie was diagnosed with autism in her sixties after a lifetime of not knowing why she felt different to everyone else. In her story she talks about the importance of realising how we all learn and think differently and that with the right adjustments, self-belief and resilience, we can all achieve what we wish for.

Looking back, I have a lot to thank my mum for. She had a tough life but worked hard and battled through her obstacles. Despite her education being disrupted by the outbreak of the Second World War she went on to work all day in an office and then walked to evening classes during the blackouts, her stomach almost empty due to the food rationing that was in place at the time.

That determination won through though and she worked her way up the ranks from Junior Clerk at the age of 14 to PA and eventually a highly respected Head of Department post in a local college. I'm telling you this because she passed this work ethic and determined attitude on to me and for this I remain truly grateful.

"You can do anything if you set your mind to it," she would regularly tell me.

As a child, I would argue that I couldn't possibly grow wings to fly to the moon or become fluent in Japanese overnight. I didn't know then that I had autism and was taking what she said far too literally. But the phrase stuck in my mind and perhaps penetrated far more deeply than I realised.

~~~

From a young age it was clear that I was a bright, intelligent and curious child. Eager to learn, excelling academically and always top of the class with minimum effort. Yet at the age of five I experienced my first significant failure at school - I simply could not tie my shoelaces.

It was a real blow to my pride when I was not the first child to receive a coveted hand-made badge - a circle cut out of pale-yellow card with a safety pin taped behind, and the words "I can tie shoelaces" written on the front. I arrived home inconsolably upset and Mum reassured me that after tea she would show me how to tie shoelaces. I could hardly wait.

Enthusiastic and confident of success, I watched as my Mum tied a piece of string round a small wicker basket handle and made a bow. I tried and tried. The string fell out of my hands every time. I must have cried.

I never really become angry, even now, but I have cried tears of frustration on so many occasions when my efforts at co-ordination or motor skills have failed. I cry at the injustice of achieving nothing at the end of what seems like an enormous effort.

My mum persisted with the shoelaces and insisted I did the same. It was no good.

Grandma tried, then Nanna - to no avail.

They were all puzzled as to why such an intelligent child could not do this one simple task.

~~~

In those days - the 1960's - children were classed either as "normal" or "backward". I had no problems academically so everyone was baffled as to why I couldn't tie my shoelaces.

Days passed and most of my classmates received their badge.

I did not.

I was probably teased and laughed at but what I clearly recall is that I was so aware that I couldn't do something - despite trying desperately hard - and it all seemed so unfair.

Eventually I agreed to leave the shoelaces and we found ways around the situation instead. In summer I wore sandals and in winter my parents would tie my shoelaces in a double knot.

Before PE (Personal Education/Sports lessons) on Thursdays I untied the knot (I had no problem doing that bit) then pulled my laces as tightly as possible and stuffed them down the sides of my shoes.
If only there had been Velcro fastenings in those days. Those sticky fasteners would really have helped me!

~~~

As an adult I chose my footwear carefully, wearing slip on shoes or those with buckle fastenings. This of course greatly reduced the choice of styles but that was practical for me, and fashion has never interested me anyway.

Well into adulthood I realised that I was no longer experiencing these significant problems with tasks that needed body co-ordination. At first I put it down to the fact that I generally avoided these things, like dancing or sewing, but I was sufficiently intrigued to try shoelaces again. I asked my sister Susan, who was teaching her son the same task, to show me what to do. Very slowly. Step by step. And I wrote it down. So now I had written instructions to take away and practise with.

~~~

By this point in adulthood, I had subconsciously discovered the best way to learn things. I need three elements - detailed written instructions, silence, and unlimited time. I have since learnt that all people are different. Some people benefit from visual information, others with repeated tasks or written practice.

Susan was incredibly patient as I wrote down the steps and practised each one from my written guide. I had copied it all out neatly with spacing and put it on my dining table.

This is what I wrote:

1. Ensure that the two lengths of lace are equal and hold them vertically and parallel.
2. Take the right side and cross it over the left side about half way up with the right side nearer to me. Hold the cross firmly between my right index finger and thumb.
3. Put my left hand through the loop moving it forwards from my body, and grab what is now the top left.
4. Pull that back through the loop towards me and pull both ends firmly outwards to form the base of the "knot".
5. Next use over half of the right-side lace to form a loop in the shape of a bunny's ear. Hold the base of the ear tightly between my right index finger and thumb.
6. Using over half of the left side lace, form a loop in the shape of a bunny's ear. Hold the base of the ear tightly between my left index finger and thumb.
7. Take the right ear and cross it over the left ear about halfway up with the right ear nearer to me. Hold the point where the ears cross firmly between my right index finger and thumb.
8. Push my left index finger and thumb through the loop at the base, moving forwards from my body and grasp what is now the left ear.
9. Pull it back through the loop towards me then pull both ears tightly outwards to form the bow.
10. Heave a sigh of relief and celebrate!

If you did manage to read all of that then you are probably wondering how complicated it all sounds, but now you can see how much harder I have to work at things most people take for granted. I still need limitless patience, practice and perseverance for these kinds of tasks.

What I had to do with the shoelaces was to follow the first instruction and practice it over and over until I felt confident enough to move on to the second instruction. Then I would do the same again, putting together a sequence and constantly consulting my notes. If I tried to move on too quickly it would all backfire, everything would scramble in my brain and I would have to return to step one. But, as I achieved each step and a small sequence started to appear, I was thrilled with the progress I was making.

All of this practice also had to take place in total silence because any kind of noise distracted me when I needed to concentrate deeply. When something is so difficult, success is much the sweeter.

I practised tying shoelaces many times each day for many weeks until it became a natural and automatic action. And actually, once I'd mastered it, I did wonder why I had found it so difficult. Maybe what I had to do was create new pathways in my brain, something which takes time and effort, but once they exist I can do things as easily as neurotypical people. In fact, my struggle with shoelaces has provided several positive outcomes. Firstly, it has made me more understanding of people who struggle with tasks. Whether it be reading or numbers or co-ordination or confidence, public speaking or just day to day problems. Secondly it has encouraged me to try and help others by thinking about different learning methods and breaking down tasks. I was able to help a friend's daughter with her times tables by chanting sums aloud during a daily walk. Thirdly, I have learned that I CAN achieve, and that has boosted my own confidence hugely.

I went on to join a tap-dancing class, explaining to the teacher that although I had autism I could catch up through home practising by watching the others and making notes to follow.

Finally, I think back to my mum's words, "You can do anything if you set your mind to it," and realise that yes, I can.

For me, certain things will always take much longer to learn, and will have to be learned with my own special technique of written instructions, silence and slowness but I can learn and make progress to compensate for my differences.

I don't have learning disabilities but I do have learning differences. Don't we all?

I celebrate my amazing autistic brain for the incredible things it can do. I am able to achieve so much in many areas of life, working around what sometimes feels like insurmountable barriers.

You really can do it.

Know that you can.

~~~**~~~

Man of Steel *by Shaun*

Shaun is 29 years old and was diagnosed with autism when he was 25. He has struggled with his mental health for many years and had a number of psychotic episodes, usually triggered by overwhelm and stress. His special interests of writing and superheroes have been stress-inducing at times but have also been a positive coping strategy for the down days. Ultimately they inspire him in his understanding of the world and in the achievement of his own life goals.

Two years ago, I had my best idea ever.

I'd wanted to be a writer for quite some time. When I was seven years old, I wrote a story at school - a rip-off of **"Power Rangers"** with a title I've long since forgotten. It featured a team of five heroes, each with a different-coloured costume. There were three boys and two girls. The only real difference was that while the Power Rangers were all teenagers, my superheroes were still at primary school. One of them being me.

But this was not the best idea I'd ever had and eventually there came a point when I stopped enjoying writing so much. By Year 6 in school I fleetingly chose to become something else - a wrestler - before returning to my interest in writing whilst at sixth form college.

The Easter during my first year there I read "Less Than Zero" by Bret **Easton Ellis** and discovered that the author had studied creative writing as an undergraduate.

I now knew what I wanted to study at university. But this was not a great idea either.

When I was at university I wasn't exactly prolific. Don't get me wrong, I handed all of my assignments in on time, I just didn't quite possess the dedication that being a writer requires. And by the time I'd finished my degree I'd given up writing completely.

Why?

Some would say laziness, but a big part of it was a lack of self-belief. Despite generally receiving good marks, I just didn't believe I had 'it'. There seemed to be a big gulf between the writers I admired and my own writing. My spirit was broken.

I had also experienced a psychotic episode the summer before my third year. This hadn't helped my confidence much but having psychology treatment and getting stuck into a bit of acting eased the pain. I was even hoping to receive a postgraduate place at a drama school - but things got really messy. I became really anxious. I couldn't leave the house for a long time and not feel as though everyone was talking about me. Not exactly ready for an acting or a writing career.

People have said human beings are incredibly good at adapting so now, not being able to act, I returned to writing, resuming work on a novel - one I hadn't really got anywhere with previously. Something was gnawing at me, though. I'd noticed that good writers tend to be skilled at talking about stories; not just writing them. About topics such as theme and symbolism. I remember one of my university tutors once saying that all great writers are great readers. After all, how do you learn the craft of writing? Even when studying a creative writing degree, you have to read other people's writing.

A shame, then, that the most profound thing I was ever able to say after reading someone else's work was, 'I really liked it.' Determined to change, I ended up reading a book on writing. It was called "Reading Like a Writer" by the fittingly named Francine Prose (see glossary). It was basically a book encouraging close reading, featuring chapters on topics such as character, dialogue, and Chekhov (see glossary). I got so much thrill out of analysing books and short stories; I ended up attempting to close-read comics and even films as well. I was determined to be able to talk about stories but ended up just talking a load of nonsense really.

I was getting stressed again.

~~~

It's worth pointing out here that I love superheroes. For a long time, superhero fiction has been my favourite story genre. However, despite its popularity, there's always been a certain amount of stigma around it - whether that is claims of it being solely for kids or just being too plain silly. People often give the impression that superhero stories lack depth and are merely fun at best. That they don't really mean anything. I personally don't mind anything being just fun, but the idea that my favourite story genre was inferior in some way played on my mind. Can't *"Dark Knight Returns"* be as good as *"Jane Eyre"*?

When I was reviewing and analysing other people's books, my close reading got out of control. I became obsessed. It had become all-out over-analysing. My brain felt like it was driving along the wrong side of the motorway at full speed.

At first I didn't mind; it was fun and exhilarating and I just thought I was on my way to becoming a writer but I started to get some odd ideas and my mum started to get concerned.

One of these ideas was that I thought the 2013 *"Superman"* film was about autism. In the film, Clark Kent/Superman's adopted father Jonathan, repeatedly talks to him about how he doesn't think the people of Earth are ready to know that someone of Clark's super-powered nature exists. Which got me thinking. Autistic people often have special abilities, whether that be a heightened sense of smell, incredible memory, or whatever else. Is this something we should hide? Or isn't the world ready? Whatever the answer was, I couldn't wait to tell my mum about my discovery: *"**Man of Steel**"* was about autism!

Initially I thought my mum just didn't understand my ideas but these grew in my mind and I started to question other people's intentions. Why were people writing these stories? I began to analyse everything with a sense of growing suspicion and things stopped being fun again. Before things got too bad my mental health team stepped in. They advised me to take a break from superheroes and writing. I found this incredibly hard at first, but I did actually want to enjoy my special interest again, not be terrified by it.

Eventually I started reading for fun again, but this led to a surprise. As much as all that close reading had messed up my brain for a little bit, it actually left me with a genuinely improved understanding of storytelling. Maybe you can relate "Man of Steel" to autism. It just doesn't necessarily mean the filmmakers did so when they were creating the film - people can have all sorts of different interpretation of things.

~~~

Looking back at those years I probably knew a lot more than I thought about superheroes and many people used to say I was a bit of a superhero expert even back then. But rather than being a negative thing, I believe the problems I had with my mental health allowed me to some degree to develop greatly as a reader and writer.

A psychologist asked me a few years ago why I like superheroes and in particular, *Batman*, my favourite. I gave an answer about him being exciting, and how his stories can be light (as seen with the Adam West-starring show from the '60s) or dark (the most modern interpretations). Yet, whilst there was a certain amount of truth behind my response, even I knew when saying it that these aren't the main reasons why I love Batman so much. But I couldn't pin it down.

Fortunately for me, the psychologist could.

"Is it because he's inspiring?" she asked.

I didn't take too long to ponder before realising she was right. What's not inspiring about a crime-fighter who refuses to kill? Come to think of it, don't most superheroes save lives while refusing to kill? Doesn't that make all of them inspiring too? And doesn't that mean something?

So, I decided to turn my novel into a superhero story.

The best idea ever that I mentioned right at the start of this story. The greatest part is that all the time I spend reading comics ... it now counts as research!

~~~

Superheroes have definitely inspired me.
They have inspired me to write.
They have inspired me to chase my dreams.
They have inspired me to try my hardest to make my life feel as though it has meaning.

And now, when I read superhero comics, or watch them on TV or in films, I'm filled with hope. That even, when life stinks, things can get better.

And when I daydream about the idea of someone reading a superhero novel of my own and being filled with those same feelings?

Well, I think that also means something.

~~~***~~~

Journey's End *by Kevin*

Kevin was 46 and 3/4 when he got his diagnosis of autism, after many years of feeling "different" and experiencing trauma both as a child and as an adult. His story shows how his local community in the 1970's and 1980's had no tolerance for difference in any of its myriad shapes or forms, and how this has impacted him. He also talks about his struggle with getting an education and employment in which he could achieve his potential.

M y autism journey began at birth.

After many years of feeling "different", I finally got a diagnostic assessment with its positive outcome at the age of 46 and three quarters. I see myself as one of the "lost generation" – a child of the 1970s, a teen in the 1980s - and ever since I have been trying to find myself. Trying to find a "cure" for something that has always been there, something I now realise that I should be embracing and using for the positive.

~~~

It's never been easy, being me, in the negative "conform or else" world that I have lived in. I was born in Oxfordshire in 1970 - the product of pushy, perfectionist, aspirational, arrogant and academic parents with militaristic and Victorian attitudes, who believed all of the authority in society is right and good, whilst making no attempt to understand the modern world and its social changes.

They were also much older than my peers' parents, and both came from very humble and poor working-class backgrounds who, with the educational and employment opportunities of post war Britain, plus plenty of thrift, worked their way up. I can remember they used to read the Daily Mirror before switching permanently to the Daily Mail. Going up in the world.

I also had an older sister who was my complete opposite – a perfect, school loving studious girl who could try her hand at anything and do well. I had to live in her shadow and at times she'd openly ridicule my eccentricities, with parents' and teachers' approval. We were chalk and cheese and there was never any sort of close relationship between us.

I later gained a brother-in-law, a qualified nurse who was lecturing students on the causes of psychological problems. Yet to me he was always very cold, arrogant and patronising and belittled me many times. We've never got on either.

The family would often shout, scream and despair at me, often over what I couldn't do, which sometimes could turn into wouldn't do, and just made me dig my heels in more. This could be from never learning to swim or ride a bicycle, my faddy eating habits and a stubborn refusal to eat "proper food", watching too much TV, not joining in and playing properly with other kids, taking little interest in my school work which led to my later academic under-achievements.

I'd often get "I can't believe a boy who can't...", and "why do they always pick on you...you really do bring it on to yourself".

I never could multi-task anything well, which is often why I struggled to do things. I did attempt to learn - first the recorder, then the violin, having lessons in these just to please my parents, but I just could not master them and my interest in them soon disappeared.

I joined a badminton club, with similar results. Worst, I joined the Cub Scouts just to please again, even though I hated the uniform and the other children.

I just wasn't interested.

It wasn't for me.

Another failure.

~~~

From an early age at my playgroup I preferred to arrange toys than to interact, often being in my own world. I continued in my own world at primary school, made more of an outcast as I hated football and was hopeless at all sports and physical games. On my final day at Primary every kid had received at least one of the certificates in swimming, athletics and/or gymnastics, except for me.

I stood out like a sore thumb.

What a disaster I was.

~~~

I struggled both with teachers and my peers throughout my education. The teachers despaired at my lack of interest and attention in class, humiliating me over my work and lack of social skills, often to the soundtrack of sneers, sniggering and vile whispers. I'd be reduced to tears or angry outbursts and given extra homework or kept in over break times. They would often moan things like "you're too slow", "shows how stupid you are", "everyone else enjoys this except you", "kids half your age can do this better" and, most notably "why do things have to be explained to you another way?".

I'd often get into trouble with the dinner ladies too. Early on it was over my refusal to eat their school dinners as my parents tried to get them to persuade me into healthier eating. Later it would be over my lack of social skills, poor manners and eating habits, "being cheeky" and fighting back against pupils, both boys and girls from lower years, always pushing their luck with "that skinny boy" who was me.

One of my former Headmasters said I needed to "stop having fits" which actually were autistic meltdowns reactive to the stress I was experiencing.

Unsurprisingly, I was often classed as "difficult".

~~~

Whilst at secondary school I was never any good at any art and crafts or creative subjects. I was hopeless at most physical sports too and the ones that I was good at failed because I never got the chance to show it, as I was always the last to be picked or partner-less and so had to miss out. I was heckled a lot by the other children, always in front of teachers, when I was trying or doing what I could do well, so then I'd get nervous and make mistakes.

Nothing worked.

Neither was I a natural in areas such as English Comprehension essays and exercises. I'd always struggle when others did well naturally (I just didn't understand emotions or words from a passage for example) and was told that I "let myself down" and I'd suffer stress because of it in class.

I could never master Comprehension in a post-war education system which often seemed to be set up to fail me.

Contrary to popular belief about people with autism and their talents, maths was another major area where I struggled. All the other pupils would say "it's easy" - they couldn't understand how I could get even the basics wrong. Worse, this was a subject I'd often be pressured about by my parents, making me struggle and stress out even more.

I hated all the timetables too and having to change classrooms and subjects for different periods each day - being expected to simply multi task and re-set my mind every hour.

Having the timetables changed each academic year was hard too. When I voiced these difficulties I was called "lazy" amongst other less than complimentary things.

~~~

Over the years, the issue of my schooling would cause many arguments with my parents. I regarded homework as a hated inconvenience which interfered with me wanting to differentiate my home life in my own world from school. I'd tear my stinky uniform from my body as soon as I got home. I hated it.

There were many times that I was too afraid to either ask for help or show knowledge for fear of retribution. Often I'd only have to speak and the other kids would make sneering noises and laugh at me, usually in front of teachers who did nothing or just told me to "ignore it".

When I had to stand up in class and read, this happened too. It was many years before I was confident enough to speak in front of a crowd again. I'd also suffer constant relentless taunts for "talking posh"; my parents believed in talking the "Queen's English" and as a result, my speech started to suffer and I developed a significant stammer at the age of 14.

I was never any good at telling jokes, worse at understanding them. I could take things too literally sometimes and I'd never realise when I was the butt of the joke. Some children would just ask me to speak, then laugh horribly at my innocent reply. I'd never know why, but I knew it wasn't kind.

I sadly suffered many physical and sexual assaults that were ignored by teachers. Others would do things to start fights with me, including kids from the lower school years.

I didn't like violence or fighting, didn't know how to hit properly and was short and scrawny-looking and seemed very young and innocent for my age. Even the girls would start punching my arms whilst all the others just smirked and looked on.

"Don't talk to Kevin, he just daydreams all the time, he isn't cool."

I can often remember them saying this whilst trying to corrupt another boy or girl I was already (or might have a chance of) getting along with. Soon that pupil would be brainwashed by the pack mentality and I would be alone yet again.

My other offences at school included not wearing designer clothes, being too nice and polite, not being interested in the sports and TV, having no knowledge of or interest in sex and a total lack of any social skills. Add to that the stigmas for not being popular, not liking noise and an inability to relax around people.

I'd also "get in the way" all the time. This was often because I couldn't steer things properly - I walked out in front of others, appeared straight out of nowhere into them or arrived suddenly round a blind corner. I might stop abruptly and start to fiddle with something when everyone else was walking. Little did I know it then that often my body moves faster than my brain thinks on situations, my brain and body don't work in time together.

Most notably, I also had many so called "stimming" habits, many of which I would do and act out without realising I was doing it. I'd often try not to, and I never understood why. These would include wringing my fingers around, picking at parts of my body, talking to or humming to myself, running and slapping my thighs, not walking in a straight line, walking hunched, or just being in a daydream, amongst many others.

I'd be subjected to smirking stares, exaggerated "this is you" impersonations to a baying crowd and when asked why I did this and I'd say I didn't know, I'd be told "you must be spastic then".

Then I'd go on to get vile impersonations and gorilla impressions.

I'd do these stimming habits at home too and have more criticism from my parents. My "mooching about" was an issue to them and the attempts they made to stop these things only made matters worse and made me do them even more. Any label they put on me would spread into the whole town and be shared regardless of age and school they attended. I'd just innocently pass another school or walk down a street and strangers would sometimes shout abuse and make gestures at me.

~~~

The town in which I lived then was a small town of narrow-minded people, in a county with many other similar towns which hide behind their tourism images. Luckily I escaped in 2000.

My parents firmly believed in a "Boys' Own" world of just overcoming and ignoring this vile bullying that I was enduring, and would criticise me instead, as if all the bullying was my fault. This was why as time went on, the family would be the last people I'd take any problems to. I'd be told not to "bottle things up" but I had no choice as their response made me feel worse.

At 15, I actually cracked from the constant bullying, both at school and at home and ran away from home. My school referred me to psychologists who were really of no help and made things much worse. This included trying to force me into speech therapy, saying that I "must have confidence in myself" and they made me go to a "Thursday group" where I'd meet up with other kids "with problems". Whilst there I was criticised again for not being outgoing enough or being relaxed around people, as if I was not trying and should instantly change. This caused much friction with my parents, who took too long to see the damage it was doing, and did, to me in the long term.

Sadly, in 1985, autism had a very, very narrow meaning. It would be 10 years before I sought counselling again, as my confidence in these professionals was destroyed. Actually, for many years I'd be in and out of counselling and not once did autism get mentioned, even some 30 years later.

At age 16 I was expected to know who I was and what I wanted from life. I was made to complete career forms at my school which failed to offer any insights or support. My parents would moan at my having no skills or hobbies that were useful in any way to a workplace.

Following pretty bad careers advice, I completed the first year of a Business Studies course at a local college which I was totally unsuited to; I couldn't grasp or understand anything they tried to teach me. What's more, my personality really was not suited to the world of business and unsurprisingly I totally failed the course and by then decided that I now had had enough of education. Sad to add that even there I suffered a sexual attack as well as homophobic bullying and taunting. I was a whole lot under-prepared for the outside world too. I had done some work experience in a library when I was at school and in an office when at college; I didn't really do myself justice in either of those places.

I had a spell of unemployment for a few months after leaving college and I still had no idea what I wanted to do. I seemed to lose myself in my own world, causing many rows and despair with the parents.

I've also always had some **Obsessive Compulsive Disorder** traits, which started when I was a teenager and reached its worst peak during this period. I have never been able to be entirely free of it.

For the next five years, into my early twenties, I unsuccessfully had a go at many jobs. Jobs that I can now see were totally unsuitable for someone like me. Jobs like admin back-office jobs and warehousing. At one point I was moved from a firm's office to its warehouse to "make me more outgoing". Unsurprisingly this had quite the opposite effect. It was a very strong lads' environment and I was accused of "not being a team player" and having "no sense of humour". I became even more withdrawn as a result.

On being fired from one of my many admin jobs I was told I, "could not cope with responsibility".

~~~

In all these jobs I continued to struggle socially both in and outside of the workplace. In my county during the 1980's and 1990's there were no suitable social clubs or hobby societies to join, none at least which reflected my interests. I never felt safe anywhere socially, so withdrawing into my own world was the key to survival.

At the age of 22 in 1992 I went to university. Again, I didn't fit in. I obsessively threw myself into my course work and somehow completed the course and passed. The one thing I did get out of Uni was to discover the friendlier and warmer communities of the North East. I tried to settle there, in Newcastle, and managed to get myself a secure furnished council flat. Unfortunately there were few suitable jobs, and help for vulnerable people like me was minimal.

I had learned to drive and passed my test when I was 19, but I never really wanted to learn from the start, and I only did so due to pressure from my then employers and my parents. I never enjoyed driving as I had to concentrate so much as well as work the car's mechanisms simultaneously. I found it impossible to relax when I did it and worse, I was subject to much road rage and taunts from work colleagues for being a cautious careful driver. I knew I wasn't cut out for the roads.

~~~

Shortly after gaining an NVQ2 in IT via Employment Training, I made the biggest mistake – I moved back home and in with my parents. I did some administrative jobs and somehow managed to hold one down in the back office of a bank for a few years, but in all the jobs I did I still suffered the same social struggles and smalltown prejudices of last time. Plus, whilst at home, old wounds and frictions with the parents re-emerged.

I'd struggled with and been unsuccessful so many times when it came to things like job interviews, no matter how many self-help books and classes I had tried. When I got offered a job at the bank's Manchester branch, I soon made the break. I had visited Manchester two years' prior and whenever I had time off work I would go and stay at a Northern or Midlands city, no matter how unglamorous it sounded.

I had discovered things about myself when in the North East, and I preferred Northern ales, communities and culture, their passion for sports such as football plus their accents and stories, friendlier people and cheaper living. No wonder I was sad to leave to go home when my holiday was over.

The job in the Manchester bank didn't work out too well but I loved and stayed in Manchester. After that I worked – all in admin jobs - for a major Insurance firm in Manchester, a corporate bank's offices and latterly a travel firm in Bolton for a record eight years until 2016. I lived in house shares throughout this time as they were all I could afford.

I've been best suited to admin jobs, dealing with paperwork and data inputting. But still in all of these jobs I struggled socially, often due to my worrying too much about what people thought of me.

I have never forgotten the bullying I endured over those years. The deep long-term pain is impossible to forget, with my confidence shattered. All sorts of things still trigger reminders for me, a random object or a particular place I might go to, or something I see on the media.

Sometimes, as a result of past trauma, I would have outbursts in the work place; caused now I know by pent-up frustrations, personal things I was having to deal with alone and the stress I had carried for so many years.

These environments and experiences have hugely impacted my mental health and caused me to self-harm over the years in various ways, either privately (which I somehow survived), or publicly as my way of crying for help - usually dismissed by others with a "don't be silly" response. It's not that I haven't tried. I have tried so hard. Socially I have joined organisations, clubs and quiz teams. But none of these things ended with me finding any real close friends, and yet again I'd retreat to the much safer place of my own world, often asking why.

~~~

My road to finally seeking a diagnosis for autism came via an unconventional route, with a breakdown and total burnout in 2016.

I had been working for a great family run travel firm for seven and a half years, until a minority of directors sold an already profitable firm to a corporate company. They then moved the company much further away, re-styled the building to an open-plan office and a strained atmosphere replaced a family one, division replaced togetherness. The one colleague that I got on with was moved away and I was once again isolated. (I'm pleased to say I'm still in touch with that colleague who has since left the firm, speaking up for me before he did. A real mate).

On Christmas Eve 2015 I had a meltdown and totally collapsed with exhaustion. I asked myself, "Why do I struggle with change, any change and even more so at this level?"

I had been seeing the company's counsellor for longer than the managers' normally approved, but autism was never mentioned as a possible solution to these lifelong problems of mine. Round and round in circles I went. I then remembered something I had read in a magazine about autism and that a new drama was due to start on the BBC called "The A Word".

Suddenly I saw myself.

~~~

I discreetly completed a self-assessment via the internet at work.

It was there - everything fell into place.

I had all the traits.

From my constant social communication and interaction struggles (I never understood "the unwritten rules"), my sensory difficulties, literal interpretation of things, my dislike of the sound of certain words - it was all there.

I have had many special interests over the years which have been absorbing and of real interest to me throughout my life. I knew many car makes and models when a child but I never cared how a car actually worked. I can still talk in depth and detail about football trivia pre-1992, but I can't play. I still know and love finding pop music chart statistics and old obscure British TV and films. I'm proud to say that I once received an acknowledgement for trivia supplied for a book about 1974.

I collect many things and like to find out more, from British comics to old magazines, to CDs of lesser known and non-hit records of the 1960s, 70s and 80s. I love old DVDs of lesser-known UK films, which are all very good for discovering interesting social history.

I've always struggled with and still have problems understanding friendship, with all its do's and don'ts. I guess I never really knew or valued what friendship was in the past and I really am sorry to anyone

I may have accidentally offended.

I'm still trying to discover what love and friendship is, as I'm still trying to find myself today. I've also always struggled to relax, especially when I'm around people.

I'm not sure I know how to.

~~~

I still have varying degrees of Obsessive Compulsive Disorder (OCD). I have had, at various times and in varying degrees, "rituals" and been very superstitious about certain things, including words and images.

My mind often wanders off on a tangent, even when I'm trying hard to concentrate on things and there are many times my mind won't stop buzzing, including thinking about trivia and number statistics, even when I'm sleeping.

But getting the diagnosis proved awkward, not helped by my GP surgery initially losing the referral. It was a tricky time - I broke my arm, was made redundant by the travel company, experienced the loss of my father, and got stuck in the mire of applying for benefits.

As most people know, there are long waiting lists for adult autism diagnostic assessments and it was a tough wait. But I did meet someone else with autism who very helpfully pointed me in the direction of community support. My GP also prescribed me anti-depressant medication which I think got me through that difficult time.

~~~

At last, in late 2016, I had the diagnostic assessment for autism and finally got confirmation a few weeks later. Finally, after all those years I was starting to get the help I needed, and I was strongly advised to consider leaving my current job, to repair my mental and physical health.

Years of uncertainty, long hours and pressures, the pain of office politics and the horrors of travelling journeys to work seemed at an end. I felt totally burned-out.

I was given help with benefits and attended some very useful post diagnostic support sessions where I met many other people with autism and we shared our stories. I wasn't alone anymore.

Since then I have joined other community support groups, most notably creative writing groups. I've had some pieces published. I've spoken publicly at events about my journey to diagnosis of autism and I've finally regained my confidence about speaking in front of others after 30 years! It's a huge milestone.

I've also been very fortunate to reside in supported accommodation, which gives me the independence that I need but also offers support when I need it. People say I've got an amazing photographic memory and that I can soak up trivia like a sponge. They say I've got an amazing and expressive voice and that I should be using it much more.

I want and hope to use my experiences to help others in some way. After years of people criticising and highlighting what I can't do, I'm discovering what I can do and being appreciated for it in a positive way. I'm finally reaching peace of mind after years of trying to conform into places and communities that simply don't suit me. I'm meeting amazing positive people and getting real help.

I'm not alone in this anymore. I have hidden talents I never knew. I'm a survivor and I want to use these things for my wellbeing and to help others too.

A long, long journey is finally showing signs of positively ending.

~~~***~~~

Theme Two: **Me, Myself and I**

Calling a Truce _by Mark_

Mark is 28 years old and was diagnosed at the age of 25. In his poetic story he talks about identity and how autism relates to his own sense of self.

The most important thing I ever learned about autism
Was that autism itself is not defined by a chain of people's similar
Yet "different" behaviours.
Autism can be anyone.
Can happen to anyone.
Because
It is defined by you
And it is a means of calling a truce
And being able to explore why you struggled all your life
With one particular, almost invisible thing.
It's about knowing how to overcome
But most importantly
Why.

~~~***~~~

The Right to Be Me by Cathy

In her story, Cathy talks about the impact of a late diagnosis (aged 36) on her mental and physical health. She spent many years trying to find the source of her ill-health whilst being disbelieved by health professionals. The public assumptions that exist about autism suggested to her that if she had a partner or a job she couldn't possibly have autism. She struggled to hold down employment because of the impact of un-diagnosed autism on her health and the effect this had on her mood, mental health and quality of life.

Cathy's story also highlights how differently autism can present in girls and women and how often they remain un-diagnosed or don't get a diagnosis until later in life.

For a long time, I didn't think I was autistic, I thought I was ill.

I really was ill. I had been in and out of doctors' surgeries since my late teens and early twenties. **Irritable Bowel Syndrome**, urinary infections one after the other, severe fatigue, brain fog, abdominal pains, constant colds, stomach bugs, strange allergic reactions, blurry vision, wounds that wouldn't heal. I had a list of symptoms across several sheets of A4 paper. But until I was diagnosed with **endometriosis** when I was 27, they could never pinpoint what was wrong. The tests usually came back clear. One doctor said that I, "didn't look like someone who is ill". I was too young, had a good job, was too well presented, my clothes too nice.

When I was 31 I was eventually diagnosed with **Chronic Fatigue Syndrome** but it still felt like the professionals weren't taking me seriously. They would sympathetically say things like, "I'm sure these symptoms are real to you…", and then do nothing. No treatment, no advice, nothing. I began to question myself. I would feel like my legs were going to give way when I was walking short distances. I would get black spots and floaty things in front of my eyes and thought I was going to pass out.

When I was still working I used to regularly say to my dad and my partner that I wasn't sure how I was going to make it home from the train station. If people came to visit our flat I would often throw the keys down from the balcony so that they could let themselves in because I didn't feel like I could manage the flight of stairs. My partner had to carry me to bed sometimes. When my exhaustion was at its worst, I used to feel as if I might not wake up again if I went to sleep. I was virtually housebound. But still I used to question if it was really happening.

Did I really feel like that or was I just making it up?

How could I be making it up and not even realise?

Was I mad?

I very slowly realised that I needed to find out what was going on for myself, because no-one was going to help me. I suspected that the health professionals thought I was a hypochondriac or perhaps just neurotic so I read everything I could find about Chronic Fatigue Syndrome and I got copies of all my lab results. Eventually I found out that I had a lot of nutritional deficiencies the doctors had missed. I read everything I could find about that, and I tried to correct them. And I thought that was the answer, and for a while it was the answer.

I managed to get to a point of feeling strong. I started running again, further and faster than I ever had. I got back to work. But it was only for a short time before my health would crash again. This cycle repeated itself many times. I would get back to work for a while, crash, and even have to leave my job because I wasn't functioning anymore. I just didn't understand it, I was eating well, taking my vitamins, looking after myself but the time I was able to stay in each job got shorter and shorter.

In order to be able to manage work, I had to say no to everything else. I stopped going out, I stopped making plans, I stopped speaking to friends. I didn't have the physical or mental energy for anything.

I had no life.

~~~

As I learnt more about the nutrients in which I was deficient, I learnt they were all nutrients that were depleted by severe and chronic stress. This never made sense to me. I didn't think I experienced any more stress than anyone else, in fact on the surface I probably had a lot less. We don't have children, my job shouldn't have been so stressful that it made me ill, I had a supportive partner plus I ate the same things, drank the same things, did the same things as my partner and friends, but I was the only one who was getting repeatedly ill.

I once did a **genetic test** which told me I had genetic mutations that affected how I absorbed certain nutrients. For a while this made a lot of sense to me but then I read about epigenetics and how your environment affects your gene expression, and once again it led me back to stress.

It took me years to fully realise that the stress was coming from being autistic and un-diagnosed.

It's strange because I remember having a conversation with my mum in her kitchen when I must have been about 24 or 25 years old. I told her that I thought I might be autistic because I found trying to fit in at work and with friends very difficult and draining. But I remember saying that it must be 'very mild autism' because I had a job, and I had a boyfriend and I had friends. I thought that people with autism didn't have those things.

And of course, that old chestnut of 'everyone's a bit autistic' or 'everyone is on the spectrum somewhere'.

I don't think either of us took it very seriously, and my mum didn't even know what autism was back then. During all the time I was ill, I never connected it to autism. There was nothing in the information I read about autism at the time that made me think it was fully describing me or my situation. It never totally fit. Until I was in my early 30's and by chance read something saying that autism can look different in women. That was the turning point.

I couldn't believe how much I identified with the experiences of other women on the spectrum that I read about. But I continued to keep it to myself. I was afraid that people wouldn't believe me, that they would just think that I was imagining my symptoms again because I'd read things on the internet.

When I eventually did find the courage to tell a few people that I seriously thought I might be autistic, they totally justified my prior concerns.

I was being silly, they said.

I was just "a bit depressed".

My partner and a friend were the only people who didn't immediately dismiss my discovery as lunacy. I didn't let myself fully believe it either, because I'd been told I was wrong and disbelieved so many times in my life. So, I just carried on - I tried to work, tried to keep going, tried to do everything that I was supposed to do. But I would keep getting ill. My life would completely stop, again.

And again.

And again.

~~~

One day I read about autistic burnout - and I knew this was what was happening to me. I knew then that I had to get an autism assessment to see if it really was the answer I had been seeking. I truly wasn't functioning, and it had got to the point where I really didn't want to live that life any more. I couldn't see any other option.

It's interesting, when I eventually made the decision to pursue a possible diagnosis, it still wasn't really for me - it was for other people. So that they could see what was wrong with me and why I found things difficult. Doesn't that say it all about women? Putting what other people thought of me in front of what I thought of myself. Trying to gain other people's approval. Getting a diagnosis of autism wouldn't be a shock to me, but other people might then understand.

I thought that I would get a diagnosis, get a few adjustments at work and that would be it, I would skip off into the sunset and all would be well.

It didn't really work like that.

~~~

I was referred for an autism assessment and finally, when I was 36 years old, I eventually got a diagnosis and the validation I had been seeking for so long. I initially felt a huge sense of relief - that I had an explanation for why things had always been so difficult but I wasn't prepared for how hard it hit me, how much information I would have to process to make sense of it, and how much worse things would get before they got better.

I had another big burnout from the stress of going through the diagnostic process and from feeling like I had to try yet again to convince people that I wasn't lying or mad.

After I was diagnosed I had to walk away from some members of the family because they didn't believe my diagnosis, said I was using it as an excuse. The whole experience was too much to deal with, not least because I was already at breaking point - and that's why I had wanted the diagnosis in the first place.

I remember going to see my GP after my diagnosis and telling him that I wasn't okay and that I was completely burnt out. He told me that it's fine to be autistic, lots of people are and they live their life and it doesn't have to be a problem. It became clear that a lot of people, even medical professionals, don't really understand what autistic people go through. Especially those autistic people that don't know that they are autistic until they are well into adulthood and have never had any help or explanation for their difficulties.

People don't understand what it does to you when your experiences are minimised and dismissed for so long, and by so many people, that you stop listening to yourself about what you want and need. When you have no option but to continually compare yourself to others because you don't understand why everything you are doing and saying is apparently wrong. When you try very hard to squeeze yourself into spaces that you don't fit into, because there aren't actually any spaces available where you do comfortably fit.

~~~

Before I knew I was autistic I told my family that whenever I was presented with a choice I never felt as if there was a right one for me. Each decision would be impossible to make because all the options would be slightly wrong.

How do you pick between equally wrong things? Why does nothing fit me, but it seems to suit everybody else? Why are the things that are supposed to be enjoyable, the opposite to me? Am I just being difficult? What is wrong with me?

I don't like big social events; they make me ill. I can only comfortably enjoy the company of one or two people at a time. Unless I'm outside, where the noise is more manageable and I can hear people more clearly. When there's a lot of people talking in a confined space, especially if there's background noise, I can't tell what people are saying, the noise is overwhelming.

Even when I can clearly hear words I can't always process them quickly enough to be able to join in the conversation properly. Events last far too long - I usually end up completely shutting down before the end. I get faint and **hangry** if I can't eat when I need to eat. I don't like Christmas get-togethers. I don't like big parties.

You're not allowed to say you don't like those things, that's not acceptable. But what is socially acceptable is to have to sneak outside to have a break from it or have to go into a dark room in the hotel because you're so exhausted and overwhelmed that you break down. It seems to me that it's perfectly acceptable to have a physical and mental health crisis after going to a social event, but whatever you do, don't say you that you don't want to go to it!

Don't get me wrong, I do want to celebrate important occasions; I appreciate that somebody has been generous enough and kind enough to invite me. I want to see friends and family; I want to be a part of things. I just don't want to have to pay for those things with my health.

I also understand that people don't invite you to events because they want you to suffer, it's because they don't even think about the possibility of it happening because it has never happened to them. I can see it's because they want their friends and family at their celebration, they want people to enjoy themselves, they are doing a nice thing.

Sometimes it might even be because it's just the done social expectation but if people don't understand sensory issues that they can't see or don't themselves experience, they think I am rude or antisocial if I turn down an invite.

And that's the point isn't it - people often don't see autism, but they usually see something. Something that is different. And that something is often negative. If your *sensory processing* differences aren't visible and if you can't explain them because you don't understand them either, your traits are often seen as you being difficult or negatively different.

When I was a child I would scream every day because it hurt to have my hair put into a ponytail. I was told to stop over-reacting. When I told people that the place I was in was too loud for me, I would be told that I'm not the only one that finds things loud. If I was anxious about something, I was told to calm down, I was overreacting again.

My meltdowns were perceived as tantrums and of me being difficult and badly behaved. I would be told to stop chewing things, stop singing, stop humming, stop tapping your foot. I was told I was too quiet, too shy, not confident enough, too blunt, too rude, too loud, too arrogant, too weird, too annoying.

I was being dramatic, I spoke too fast, I said the wrong thing, I was just being different for the sake of it. I was just being difficult to spoil other people's fun, or to get attention. I was just not very nice. Whatever label or personality trait you can think of that is not very complimentary, I have probably been that to at least one person in my life at some point. When you get told often enough and by enough different people that you're not okay as you are, you believe it. You do whatever you can think of to do to make yourself okay.

~~~

Before I knew I was autistic, I had never really understood how I was so many different things to so many different people. I also never really understood how I often didn't feel like the thing they were telling me I was. Some people would tell me they found it hard to believe that I was autistic as they had always thought I was 'the confident one.'

At work they told me that I was too timid, and I needed to learn to assert myself more. Other people would say that I was so assertive I was bossy. People told me I was funny and bubbly, some people thought I was serious and boring... I was very confused all the time. I eventually realised it's because I mustn't have ever really been myself. I didn't know how to be. I was trying to be what I thought other people thought I should be. Which is exhausting, and totally unachievable - how do you please everyone? Especially when you really don't understand their rules and are just scraping by with mimicry.

Outside of the professionals I met during and after my diagnosis, my partner is one of the only people that I didn't have to expend an awful lot of energy explaining autism to. I think it's because he's one of the very few people that I haven't had to pretend with. He sees what happens to me after I've done everything that is expected of me and he helps me to pick up the pieces. But what eventually did happen after my diagnosis, with the help of a few people like Helen (the author of this book), was that I started to believe myself. I started to listen to what my body was telling me, and I started to understand my sensory needs. If something felt too loud, I believed myself that it was too loud and I let myself leave. Better yet I didn't make myself go there in the first place.

- I got myself some noise cancelling headphones.
- I learnt that I need to make sure to prioritise exercise for my well-being.
- I learnt that an open plan office is really not the place for me.
- I learnt that anywhere busy or noisy is not the place for me.
- I learnt that I process information differently, and that's why I find a lot of things hard.

- I learnt that I don't do well with verbal instruction, and it's much better if I have things written down if I need to actually use and remember them. I learnt that if I have something to say I should write it down because there's a much better chance of me communicating what I actually mean than if I try to verbalise it.
- I learnt that some people will never hear what you have to say regardless of how you say it and that it's okay to stop trying when this happens.
- I started to be more comfortable asserting my needs and learning how to say no to things that will make me ill.
- I learnt that if there are people who make me feel inferior or broken, I don't have to prove myself or be good enough for them.
- I learnt that I don't need to have approval from other people at all, I just need to give it to myself.

~~~

Three years later and I'm faring much better.

It probably doesn't always look like that to the outside world, but that's because I'm learning to do the things that are important to me, not the things other people think I should be doing. I'm starting to actually understand the things that are important to me because I never knew. I've always done what's important to everyone else.

I'm doing a psychology degree part-time from home, and I am enjoying studying (see end note). I am learning a lot about the way that I work, and the things that I need to be able to work well. Previously I thought I was stupid, as I had no other reason to explain why I was struggling to function in an office. Now we're learning how to have holidays and take trips that don't bring on a major meltdown or health crisis, and that my partner and I both enjoy.

I have some nice friends who I am comfortable with, and who I walk, run, swim and cycle with when I can.

115

I have a better relationship with my parents; they have made a big effort to understand me and respect the boundaries I have put in place. I think I understand them better. I hope to eventually be able to spend time with the family and friends that I don't often see in ways that I can manage.

My physical health is much better and thankfully I'm able to be consistently active again. During the difficult lockdown periods of 2020, I was active for around 300 days of the year, even if it was just a short local walk. Exercise is very important to me, I take my running shoes wherever I go.

When I go away, the change in routine can be very unsettling and I think being able to take myself off for a run is the only way I have survived, especially before my diagnosis.

I like open water swimming because it seems to be good for my brain; the cold water helps my mood and because you can't really see or hear much in open water it calms my senses. The swimming pool is the total opposite - I find it too loud, too bright and chaotic and I often feel more anxious when I come out.

I also enjoy having an event to train for; I think I've had so much disruption and interruption to my life before I was diagnosed that it is important to me to be able to progress with something. Over the last few years I've achieved some of the goals I've had for a long time but had never been able to consider doing because my body kept breaking down. I've completed a middle-distance triathlon and one day, I will do a long course. I hope to do some more cycling trips with my partner and perhaps an ultra-marathon, as well as much more swimming outdoors. These things might not seem big achievements to some people but they are a big deal to me.

There were many times during my young adult years - my 20's and 30's - that I couldn't even get up the stairs to my flat. Exercise is what gives me energy when so many other things deplete it, and it is what has enabled me to keep going at times when I really didn't think I could.

~~~

I still have difficulties with my mental health. It looks as if I may have **Premenstrual Dysphoric Disorder (PMDD)**, a syndrome that really impacts my life at certain times of the month. It can be hard to manage.

My self-esteem needs a lot of work but at least I now recognise that. I understand more about why that is and can do something about it in time.

I still feel burnt out a lot of the time; I can cope with a lot less than I used to be able to but I've learnt that it's okay to say no to things when I need to. I cancel arrangements, I need a lot of flexibility and downtime but, I am also starting to see my positives instead of the negatives that have always been pointed out to me.

I'm slowly starting to see what my strengths are, what I might be good at, and how I learn best. I'm starting to cut myself some slack instead of beating myself up all the time and I let myself rest when I need to. It will take time, but things are improving, and I feel like I am more able to control my circumstances rather than just getting swept along in other people's lives.

And when my hormones are not causing trouble, there are a lot of times when I'm happy.

I'm not constantly overloaded anymore, and I have a nice life with my partner. I want this life that I have. Before I was diagnosed and for a while afterwards that wasn't true. I wasn't sure how I could keep carrying on when everything was such a fight.

What I find saddening in my story is that I let other people decide who I was for so long. That I had to have a piece of paper with 'Autism Spectrum Condition' written on it before I could ask for and get what I needed. And the saddest thing is ...

... until the world knew I was autistic I didn't feel that I had the right to be myself.

~~~***~~~

Note: Cathy passed her Psychology degree in July 2021 with a distinction for her dissertation.

Looking Back – Those First Few Years *by Paul*

Paul was diagnosed as an adult. He speaks about always feeling different in his childhood and how this went unnoticed by others, which he now finds baffling. As a bright, intelligent and curious child in the 1970's, he struggled to be understood by others around him and to navigate the world of school and education.

It was during the year 1969 that something terrible happened to me.

My parents abandoned me. They sent me to school. I couldn't understand the reason for this betrayal. I hadn't done anything particularly awful for a good few weeks and had even halted my in-depth investigations into swearing as a perfect art form.

I hadn't actually spoken a single word until I was nearly 4 years old, so I would have thought my family would applaud any investigations I made whatsoever into language, especially my excitingly colourful use of the most offensive cursing and blaspheming. At the age of three and a half they dragged me around various doctors and specialists because I hadn't uttered a word. They knew I had a voice - I just didn't use it.

My first word was not in fact a word. It was a full grammatical sentence. Grandma was in the back kitchen pantry putting tins away; I came up behind her with a growling tummy and pronounced, "Can I have a jam sandwich?"

With a stunned look, she agreed I could have the requested jam sandwich. She slowly turned to me, and I saw a mixture of emotions flit across her face as she proclaimed, "You little swine! You CAN talk!". This was closely followed by, "Do you know how worried we've been about you?"

The worry I caused them was somewhat eased a few weeks later when our family doctor, Dr Robinson, told my mother, "Perhaps he never asked for anything because you were such a good mother that he never needed to".

In the weeks leading up to my abandonment in school I continued to use this voice I had found. I used it a lot. Mainly through tantrums and crying fits.

But despite piteous crying and pathetic wailing, they still did it – they sent me to the horror of school. My voice didn't really help me in school. That first year was truly awful. I understood that the other kids liked to run around, play imaginary games – not me of course but I could see why they did it.

But the noise!

The screaming, the screeching, the echoing shrieks and howling caused me genuine pain, to the point that I could not withstand it. So, another coping strategy came into being – I would purposefully pull my tongue out at the teacher. I quickly learnt that this was the perfect way to get grounded in the classroom and sit quietly during playtime – perfect! Happy times.

Another blessing for me in terms of school avoidance was the weirdness of my family. Back in the 1970's they would have been called "Anti-Vaxxers" – they didn't believe in injections and immunisations so this meant that in short order I caught Measles, Mumps, Chicken pox, Rubella, Muscular Flu and Whooping Cough. The subsequent bout of pneumonia scarred my lungs for life but what a small price to pay for a glorious three weeks off school!

I didn't really make friends at school either. Only a succession of people who came to my house and messed with my stuff, touching everything, leaving toys in the wrong place. No thanks.

The jewel in the crown I remember came towards the end of the first year in school, when I arrived home absolutely crawling with head lice. I always knew school was a cesspit of filth and depravity, as I stood there ruined and infested with a head full of vermin.

"This is all your fault," I announced accusingly at home.

My family actually laughed at me.

And carried on laughing for years as each and every girlfriend I brought home was told the story.

And they still made me go to school.

Where people still didn't see me. And never did.

~~~******~~~

An Autistic Acrostic by Anonymous

This poem was scribbled on the back of an envelope. The author wishes to remain anonymous.

A loner, never part of the group
Understood by no-one, not even by myself
The odd one out, targeted by bullies
I hid away and concentrated on my studies.
Sobbing regularly, shut in my bedroom
Told off yet again for things I couldn't help
I hated myself and my clumsiness and I
Couldn't see why being truthful was ever wrong.

Drifting through life as an adult
I was happy enough on my own
Accepted by friends and safe in my routines.
Gradually I researched autism and wondered.
Now I have been diagnosed with it
Overjoyed , I understand and accept myself finally.
Silently sobbing tears of sheer relief and happiness
I feel a heavy lifelong burden lift.
Suddenly I am free - to be myself and live at last.

~~~**✱✱**~~~

A Bit Odd *by Paul*

Paul received his diagnosis at the age of 42, following a period of mental ill-health and a crisis admission to hospital. He outlines the importance of adequate funding for effective diagnostic and support teams for people on the spectrum.

I've always known I was different. It's probably my earliest memory.

I was diagnosed with autism in January 2018 at the grand old age of 42. It's the cause of much merriment to me that at no point in all of those years did anyone pull me aside and say, "You know what mate? You're ...A Bit Odd". Although, after being diagnosed, I told my brother-in-law who looked at me, paused and then said, "Ah.. that explains a lot".

They were very different times when I was young, so any signs I did exhibit as autism wouldn't necessarily have raised any concerns. Plus, I think I learned to mask my difficulties from very early on in life.

I did have a few little quirks when I was young, such as nibbling my bedding. I don't mean that I used to eat whole pillowcases or anything, I'm not that monstrous. Just all along the top edge of the bedding seam. Maybe it was a sensory thing or perhaps it soothed me. Answers on a postcard for that one please.

I was also obsessed with my grandmother's cigarette lighter. A big old thing, shaped like a flintlock pistol, purely ornamental and never actually used. I would be absorbed for hours, taking it apart and putting it back together.

Over and over again.

And still nobody wondered.

Fast forward to the time of my diagnosis and that was when so many lightbulbs went off for me. So much suddenly made sense.

It took me over a month to read and digest my diagnostic report. Getting a cold clinical list of all the ways you are not quite right is hard to take. And disclosing my diagnosis to others was sometimes tough.

I got asked so many times, "What does that mean then?". I had to moderate my autistic bluntness more than once.

I'm fortunate in that I was offered support from an ASC support team in my local area. These are few and far between, sadly. They helped me see that it's not just possible to have a life as an autistic adult, it can actually be an enjoyable one.

The present day?

I'm doing pretty damn well.

I learn more about myself and how my autism affects me all the time. I know what I can do, what I have to force myself to do, and what I struggle with. And you know what? It's all just fine.

I may be different to everyone else.

But there's absolutely nothing wrong with me.

There never was.

~~~**✲✲**~~~

Blue Flask and Sandwiches by Pamela

Pamela was diagnosed in mid-life as an adult following her retirement as a teacher. Her difficulties with physical co-ordination, sensory issues and love of routines have been significant throughout her life, however, she has been successfully able to navigate these and create a full life of adventure and joy. Her poem is inspired by "When I am an old woman I shall wear purple," by Jenny Joseph.

Now I've turned sixty
I shall wear black school trousers
And children's T-shirts.
I'll buy boys' jackets with zipped pockets and a hood
And boys' trainers with Velcro fastenings.
I'll run down the road to the newsagent's
As if I'm being chased,
And swing from the beams in my garage.
I will eat chocolate every day
And biscuits whenever I want.
I'll grumble about no bus pass till 66
And make sure I get senior discounts at museums.
I'll go out on my own to places of interest,
Ask endless questions and make copious notes
To write up and file alphabetically.
I'll take my shoulder bag everywhere
Stuffed full of things I might need.
I'll put my blue flask and sandwiches in my cat bag
Then sit down on the pavement to enjoy my lunch.
I'll talk to dogs I don't know and feed them treats
But ignore people who make polite conversation
I'll live life to the full
In my own way, in my own little world.
I know I'll be perfectly happy
Because I have been practising for years.

~~~******~~~

Theme Three: Love and Community

'He can't have autism ...' by AnnMarie

AnnMarie is mum to two boys, Byron and Lochlann, both of whom are now larger than life teenagers. Her youngest, Lochlann, is severely disabled. It has been a tough journey for AnnMarie since he was seven weeks old – for that's when he first got sick – and now at 18yrs, it hasn't got any easier, in fact, it gets ever harder. Though tired of being told how 'strong' she is, AnnMarie realises the special gift she has been given with Lochlann and, in her work as a book coach, author and publisher, she believes passionately that everyone can tell their story. She is both honoured and humbled to have been asked to be a part of this incredible book.

I was always going to have three children. That was the plan.

Well, it *was* the plan, until Lochlann came along.

Lochlann was my second pregnancy, so I was way more relaxed than my first. So much so that I barely glanced through the myriad of books and pamphlets provided by the midwives. I knew what I was doing. I'd got this.

My second son came kicking and screaming into the world on the 26th April 2005 after a relatively normal pregnancy. I'd been lucky with both my pregnancies and though I'd not encountered any problems, I was convinced Lochlann was going to be a girl because my second pregnancy was different in every way to my first (and I secretly really wanted a little girl).

I went into labour very quickly, such that baby number two was almost born in the hospital car park and, when the midwife (who had only managed to get one glove and half an apron on) held him up, it took me a moment to register that he had 'bits'. He wasn't a girl.

Anyone who has ever had a child will know that in the end, it doesn't matter a jot. You may start out wanting boys or girls, but actually, when you birth them, you don't care. You love them instantly and know that you would lay down your life for them. Little did I know just how much of my life I would lay down for Lochlann.

All was well until he was seven weeks' old, and then he began fitting. I didn't know what it was at the time and it wasn't until we ended up in a private room on the children's ward that I really considered how serious things were. He fitted almost constantly until finally, three days after arrival at the hospital, he was given the right meds to calm him. The meds worked. He stopped fitting, but they also virtually comatosed him – one of the necessary side-effects.

He was to remain on this strong medication until he was two years old, after which we were able to wean the dosage down and, when he suffered no further fits, the medication was withdrawn altogether. (Sadly, he began fitting again at six years old and now has a diagnosis of nocturnal epilepsy with daily medication).

During the first two years of his life, despite professional opinions to the contrary, it became blatantly obvious that he was 'different' and, with him being my second, I knew what he should have been doing – and thus, what he wasn't doing.

'Developmental delay,' they said. 'Very common.'

I disagreed. In my heart I knew he would never be okay. At around the same age, two years old, I questioned the experts about autism. Was it possible my son was autistic?

'No,' they said, 'he can't have autism because he makes eye contact with you'. And that was the ongoing narrative.

Because of, or perhaps in spite of my gut feeling, I wouldn't let it rest and pushed for a diagnosis. He had been hospitalised on and off with other issues and his 'differences' were mounting up. I had had enough of being told he would 'grow out of' them all and was becoming angry and increasingly despondent that my mother's instinct was being largely ignored.

Finally, we were awarded with a diagnostic assessment when he was almost three years old, and I was unsurprised to learn that he was 'severely autistic' – despite the eye contact. At that age Lochlann wasn't crawling, he was only just stable in a seated position, he wasn't vocalising, he was still in nappies - in short he was so far behind his peers that I needed something, someone to listen, and the autism diagnosis achieved that. Now, when I took him anywhere, I could say that my child was 'autistic' and that would explain to everyone why he behaved the way he did. It was also my route to support and to obtaining the right educational setting for him, although that wasn't without its difficulties.

What I had no knowledge of - and why would I – was just how hard it is to access services, get support, financial aid, advice and guidance when you have a child with special needs. The services are out there but they are limited. There is no funding. There are no staff and because each child usually needs extensive support, they can't be within a large group so more staff are needed. It's a minefield. A minefield of never-ending paperwork, phone calls, referrals, arguments, pleas ... and often things only moved forwards for Lochlann when he was blue-lighted to hospital following an incident. Then measures would be taken for additional help.

He began crawling when he was three and a half and I held a party, a crawling party, because I knew how much of a challenge that had been for him. Everyone who came had to endure the whole party on their hands and knees … because that's what life was like for Lochlann.

Around eighteen months later he began to walk, but one of his many (now diagnosed) conditions is ataxia, meaning that his balance is poor. This has contributed to severe developmental delay with both fine and gross motor skills and, if you couple that with autism and lack of danger awareness, he requires a wheelchair when outside of the home – for his own safety but also for ease. Trying to manage him when he is not 'restricted' is a nightmare. And that's probably a really un-PC thing to say, but if you're a parent of a child with Lochlann's level of severe needs, you do what you have to do to keep them safe and yourself within a hair's breadth of sane. (For reference, two years ago we were given a full diagnosis of STXBP1 following extensive genetic testing).

As a family, both immediate and extended, Lochlann's challenges have had a huge impact. His brother, Byron, was only two when Lochlann was born and so has not really known a 'normal' life. He has grown up understanding that there are some things we simply cannot do (logistically), though we have tried our hardest to give him the best version of 'normal' that we can. This meant effectively splitting our family in two and now, seventeen years after Lochlann was born, it has taken its toll. My husband and I were so used to being two different things to two very different boys that we forgot to take care of ourselves and decided to separate. The decision is amicable – but it remains a sad by-product of the situation we found ourselves in. So, what does having a child like Lochlann mean?

It is exhausting. It is endlessly repetitive. It is thankless. It is painful. It is a constant battle. It is saddening. It is isolating.

He is now a fully grown eighteen-year-old who is non-verbal, still in nappies, has limited mobility, needs full 24/7 personal care and is prone to frustration, anger and physical outbursts. These are usually aimed at me. I am covered in bruises most days. I have been hit, punched, pinched and pulled more times than I care to remember. The physical demands of managing him have exacerbated an existing chronic neck condition which means I spend most of my days on painkillers and, being on call all of the time for the last twenty years, has caused my (already poor) mental health to deteriorate rapidly. Our family is now fractured and in no way resembles the cohesive unit with three children that I naively planned (we never had the third child). I've grieved for the child I 'should have had'. I grieved for the brother that Byron 'should have had'. I've grieved for the damage to my relationship and I've lost my temper more times than I can remember with those who are trying their best but simply don't understand.

Yet, if you gave me the chance to wave a magic wand, would I take it?

No. Absolutely not.

Lochlann has no voice. He will never have a voice and that means I will be his advocate now and always. It means that now he is eighteen, I will have to get a legal document to allow me to continue to make his decisions. The path is definitely not getting easier – if anything, the road ahead is even more complex – but I still wouldn't wave that magic wand.

Because Lochlann has given me a gift I didn't even know I wanted. He has introduced me to the most amazing community of selfless and giving people. He has shown me what it is like to be different and taught me to embrace that. He has given me unconditional love in the way only a child like him can, and he has made me so proud of every step he has taken, every small achievement he has celebrated.

Without Lochlann, I truly believe I would have lived half a life. An ignorant life. I wouldn't have understood what the neuro-diverse and autistic community is like and I would definitely have been poorer for it. I would have lived in my selfish bubble, and I would have been that person who looked at someone like myself and Lochlann and concluded that his behaviour was down to 'bad parenting'. And that naivety is understandable and perfectly okay. People cannot possibly know a situation that they have never experienced and I am fine being judged - for through Lochlann I have realised that the judgement is on them, not me.

He has made me a stronger mother. A more resilient woman and through each and every test I have learned a valuable lesson. I love both my children equally. They are both incredible human beings. And I would never wish to change either of them.

I genuinely hope that this book and these stories will help others to realise they are not alone. Parenting a child with special needs is incredibly isolating. They won't get invited to friend's houses or parties … but that's okay – and over time I have come to accept this in a way which lays no blame. It's hard though, when your 'tribe' is instantly culled to almost none.

We can never know another person's life until we have walked a mile in their shoes. The people in this book who have bravely shared their stories are giving you a glimpse of what their shoes are like and for me, as a parent, I am giving you a glimpse of mine and Lochlann's too.

These people are incredible. They are selfless. They are loving and giving and they deserve every opportunity to be celebrated.

I get to celebrate and love someone just like them, every single day – and there is no magic wand that could ever recreate that.

~~~**~~~

Mr Smirnoff and the Velcro Gang by Steph

Steph is a mum to two adult children. Her son has a diagnosis of autism. She is also a co-founder of a charity that supports children and young people with neuro-developmental conditions and their families.

M otherhood.

It's a funny old game to be sure and one I came to quite late for my generation at almost 28 – and to be fair it would have been much later than that if Mr Smirnoff hadn't had a hand in it.

There's nothing you can do to prepare for (in my case) suddenly swelling to the size of Jupiter's third moon, being crap at giving birth and then experiencing the overwhelming love you immediately feel for the steaming, screaming small person who is suddenly deposited onto you. Then they send you home and you realise the image of The Royals standing on the steps of The Portland Hospital all clean and dressed and fresh looking has no bearing at all on the reality of dragging your flaccid, sore, Kaftan-wearing lump of a body across a car park, praying nothing else falls out of you before you can sit down again. There was no misty buff announcement pinned to my gatepost and I definitely, definitely did not glow at any stage of the proceedings.

By the time the first bundle of joy was 12 months old it had become apparent that he was very different from other children of the same age. In fact, I'd go as far as to say very, very different.

You shouldn't compare children – but you do, and you shouldn't read up on conditions on the World Wide Web – but you do. Then you have to turn into "that woman" in order for anyone to take you seriously, answer pregnancy and birth questions with so many people, be tested to the moon and back, tell the pregnancy and birth stories again and eventually someone will be able to tell you why your son is so different.

In our case the end of the process and the beginning of a whole new journey was one word.

Autism.

I wasn't shocked or surprised or remotely bothered. I haven't grieved for the child I never had and I'm not one bit sorry to have a child (now hairy adult) with autism because he's fabulous and glorious and hilarious and mine. I did good.

By the time bundle of joy number two arrived and made our family complete (as in I'm never, ever doing THAT again) we'd bumbled along for almost four years without much guidance or support and it was beginning to really irk me that there didn't seem to be anything on offer to do this.

Dual parenting was hard and a bit lonely and, as neither of them had the good grace to come with an instruction manual, very difficult to know if what I was doing was helping or hindering my big lad.

I didn't even know how many other families locally also had children with autism, but I hoped there would be at least another one or two.........or over 800 as it turned out.

Blimey.

So, the first charity was born in 2004 and the second (and current one) in 2012, with the specific aim of making sure disabled children and young people have a voice that is heard and the opportunity to have time and space to just be who they are.

I'm not a wait around kind of person - it's generally faster to do it yourself and, as experience has taught me, much better if you live with it as well as work with it.

Along the way I've met people who are in it for personal reasons and personal gain - you quickly learn to tell the difference between these people and those who are around because they want to help and make a difference.

You hang on to those people as tight as you can because they are the hairy bit to your spiky bit of Velcro. You also learn that actually you are an absolute nightmare to work with and you then learn to move away and dance to your own tune with your Velcro Gang.

For me, motherhood brought so much more than motherhood. It brought a whole new perspective on the world and a passion for something that pre-launch I knew absolutely nothing about.

It taught me about what achievement actually means and that no matter how "big" or "small", successes should be celebrated; the amount of effort it took to climb that particular mountain should definitely be recognised and have a big flapping flag stuck on top as a reminder.

My daughter is extremely clever and academically has already achieved great things, and that's even before she finished university (I never went - no attention span) and embarks on the rest of her life. But she works damn hard to do well.

Just as hard as my son did to learn how to use a washing machine and how to have a phone conversation and how to fasten a zip. Same amount of work, same level of success, just different spheres of aspirations. Different, not less.

I'm fairly sure my dad hovered on the autism spectrum somewhere and similarly, fairly sure my maternal grandfather did, so it's definitely in the blood.

It's also something that's been part of my life for all of my life and it makes me feel safe in its familiarity.

Autism is part of the foundations of family to me and there isn't anything I would change about it.

Why would I? You can't improve on perfection.

~~~***~~~

Wholes not Parts *by Dr Rachel Taylor*

Dr Rachel Taylor is a psychologist and researcher. She is passionate about raising the profile and acceptance of neurodiversity and has worked with many people with autism over recent years using the results of her work to inspire and inform future service providers.

Kindness is a very over-used word and misunderstood value.

Do we even know what it genuinely is to be kind anymore?

When I think about life, and I do, probably more often than I should, I constantly return to a time in my life which very possibly was the most thought-provoking, meaningful experience that I have encountered to date.

When I embarked on my work with adults who have a diagnosis of autism, I never dreamed what would unfold.

I tell everyone who will listen, that it was the most joyful, upsetting, frustrating, sad, depressing, hopeful, hopeless, invigorating work that I have ever done in my life and I do not know how that top spot will ever be replaced.

Kindness though was inherent throughout it all, from its very absence, to being misconstrued, to being the most innocent of occurrences.
I wanted to find out, in my role as psychologist and researcher, what people with autism needed to be well.

It seemed to me to be a travesty of modern times that autistic people had a mortality that was ten to fifteen years less than neurotypical people, as well as a quality of life that could be limited in scope and opportunities.

I wanted to propose themes, theories, and discoveries with the intent to facilitate better understanding, awareness and hopefully changes to how we approach and manage difference in all of society.

All the people I met with spoke of a huge weight that they endured, the responsibility for their companions in their own community and beyond. How they could feel energy and emotions which they wanted to fix but had run out of solutions. They spoke of the sheer grit and determination to get through days, weeks, and months, with coping strategies that all too often created isolation, despair, and sadness.

They remembered emotional occasions like the birth of babies, deaths of babies, relationship breakdowns, achievements both from themselves and others as if they were happening in that moment. I felt the emotions as keenly as they did, but as a researcher was compelled to not interfere with their process.

They spoke of a lifetime of being misunderstood until a diagnosis of autism was their 'a-ha moment'.

Having a label though did not mean for many that life got easier, indeed for some it got harder as their families and friends refused to believe they were that label. The label itself could also lead to separation, isolation, and judgement. It was not easy.

The ability to feel positive emotion we discussed at length, particularly the emotion 'joy'. It was remarkable really that what emerged as a key theme for wellbeing was a universal belief that joy is essential for wellness. But for some people with autism, the after-effects of joy can be hard to bear.

The very act of that spontaneous outburst of joy was enough to put some people into a deep dark depression afterwards so for many, it was simply avoided as too big a price to pay.

Kindness was often given freely by people on the spectrum, to others who were deemed in need of support and help, with no expectation that it would ever be returned to them.

I don't know what your experience of autism is as you are reading this book, whether it be a person with autism, someone who is close to someone with autism or maybe you care or work within the field of autism. Or maybe you are curious, want to learn more, want to become more aware of neurodiversity.

In any case I am not sure that it matters where you are coming from, I think it matters more to intend to support all and be kinder now and going forwards.

I am going to list some of the key lessons that I learnt from my work in the hope there may be something in there that will be of help or use to you:

- If someone is emotionally overwhelmed, you really need to allow them the space to express their emotion. During my research I learnt to sit with people emoting a whole spectrum of feelings. It was privilege and a huge gift for me to just allow people to be. It is okay to be emotional - getting comfortable with uncomfortable helps us all!
- People with autism feel. A lot. We need to be more open and direct with each other, which will also help us to be more honest with ourselves.
- Just because something says something on the tin, does not mean that it is always autism-friendly. There is not a one size fits all for any of us, including those with neurodiversity.
- People with autism put so many limitations on themselves as a coping strategy for life – try not to limit them any further. What do we need to do to support them to be the most amazing versions of themselves and allow people access to the things they need to reach their full potential?

- Think about - how open are you to different? What does it mean to you if there is difference? Is it a source of delight or a source of suspicion? Now that you have read this book what difference might it have made to your own opinions?
- Kindness is not an indulgence, nor anything to be brushed to one side. Kindness is the very essence of acceptance and inclusion. It is what we all desire and what we all need. Humans need humans, no matter what label we place upon ourselves and others. Human beings need to be human. Regardless of how their brains work.

Kindness is as complex and as simple as you make it. People with autism, as we all are, are as complex and simple as that too.

The one thing I do know is that if we are open to both kindness and difference then we can experience life in a richer, more interesting, more life-affirming, deeper and more purposeful way. We have better relationships, more meaning and acceptance both of ourselves and those we meet.

For us all to be well we need all three, in abundance. It is a mutually beneficial state, one which we all need to embrace.

I suppose then that is the essence of kindness, how well we all think of ourselves, each other and how we hold each other up in all environments.

My greatest wish is for all with autism to be wholes and not parts; for there no longer to be limitations placed upon them by social conditioning, learnt behaviour or unkindness.

And in that, we can all play a part.

~~~***~~~

When Hats are Life *by Russ Williams*

Russ Williams is a Welsh author and blogger. His story introduces his experience of growing up with a brother with autism and learning disabilities and talks about how the public perception of autism has been affected by the media, including the impact of the film, "Rain Man". You can read more of Russ' stories and blog at his website: russwilliams.org

Viejo Grunon was sitting on his usual bench by the sea in his home city of Salou, as he always did in the evenings.

The old man sat in his shorts with his legs crossed, one sandal-bearing foot swaying from side to side to the tune playing in his head. His hands were clasped together and resting on his belly, thumbs twiddling, skin dark and leathered by years of basking in the sun. He looked out at the horizon thoughtfully, thanking God for all the wonderful years and pondering what the new millennium would bring, when suddenly...

THUMP!

His peaceful moment was interrupted when something heavy landed on his head. The shock made the impact seem worse somehow, almost painful. He felt the frightening force clasp tighter around his favourite wicker hat then lift up into the air revealing his balding scalp.

Viejo covered his head and wailed; "¿Qué haces, estúpido turista inglés?!"

Looking up, he saw a young boy, younger than ten, pale and white with too much sunblock on his face. He was just standing there, holding Viejo's hat up in the air and admiring it from different angles, humming happily to himself.

Viejo hesitated. There was something 'wrong' with this boy...

141

"Sorry!" The boy's father ran over to them and handed Viejo back his crumpled hat.

"¡Mira el estado de mi sombrero!" Viejo ranted and raved, infuriated by the state of his hat.

"Sorry! Yhm... 'autistico'! Autistico!" the boy's father tried to explain in a thick, northern Welsh accent.

Then he took his son by the hand and led him away.

"¡Maldito inglés!"

~~~

You have to keep your wits about you when walking in public with an autistic brother. That incident on our family holiday back in 2000 is just the tip of the iceberg considering how many times my brother has trampled all over society's conventional rules and got himself into trouble while we're out and about.

From taking a stranger's sausage roll right off their plate in a café to breaking wind in restaurants, revealing his rear end when peeing in public toilets to having total meltdowns in theme park ride queues, sticking his finger up a ram's nose and crushing goldfish to death with their little castle, inappropriate staring and the resulting erections, attacking teachers and destroying classrooms, pushing toddlers down the stairs and strangling his cousins, my brother truly has put himself in some awkward predicaments over the years, with undoubtedly many more to come.

He loves hats, you see.

He's fascinated by all the different kinds, and he likes studying them from various angles - up close, moving them slowly into his peripheral vision without moving his eyes, bringing them over his head and around the side of his face, like he's imagining an opening scene from Star Wars, with the large spaceship replaced by a giant wicker hat.

He'll keep a hat by his side when he's watching television, he takes one to bed with him and will even take one with him on long car journeys for 'entertainment'.

So, when he saw the delight that was sitting on top of that old man's head that day in Spain, he just had to have a closer look, and for him, social boundaries are essentially non-existent.

~~~

I remember the day Mam told me that my brother was autistic. I was about five or six years old and was watching an entourage of Nineties Saturday morning kids' shows on Fox Kids and Nickelodeon - Kenan and Kel, Pokemon, Goosebumps... it was one of those seemingly endless school summer holidays when six weeks seemed like six years and the sun actually shone when it was meant to.

She came up to me, asked me to mute the telly, and sat down beside me. She said something along the lines of, "Your brother isn't like 'other' brothers...," and handed me a small pamphlet entitled something similar to what she just said, along with the subtitle, 'How to live with your autistic sibling', or something like that.

Mam seemed hesitant, and on edge - perhaps she was expecting upset and confusion, but I remember being intrigued by it all - I wasn't mortified, wasn't angry, wasn't ashamed and I wasn't apathetic towards it.

By all accounts I took that pamphlet and I read it all in one sitting, wide-eyed and full of wonder - my brother was "special", and I wanted to know more.

The pamphlet told me that my brother would never 'love' me in the conventional sense, that he would never make eye contact with me, that he would never want to be hugged or make friends, he would never have a love life, would hate crowds and loud noises, and might be exceptionally gifted in one area.

~~~

Through the years I have seen and read so many myths and misconceptions surrounding autism; the condition still baffles people today.

Mam was blamed for my brother's autism back when he was first diagnosed: "...have you ever heard of 'refrigerator motherhood'...?"

Myths about autism exist because the condition in itself can be difficult to explain and can never truly be summed up in one sentence. It is easy to explain something in a manner such as, "Oh... he doesn't have any empathy," or "He hates loud noises," but there are plenty of people in this world without empathy or who despise loud noises, but it doesn't make them autistic, and even then, not one person on the spectrum is the same as the other. All I knew about autism was what was in that pamphlet and what I saw on TV.

You've probably seen a documentary or film about autistic savants at some point - people who can remember every line from every page of every book they've ever read, who can glance at a photo of a city landscape and recreate it perfectly, or who can calculate insanely large sums in their heads within seconds. (Savants typically have another co-existing neurodevelopmental disorder, such as autism for example, and there's a one in a million chance of being born a savant, with it affecting more males than females on a ratio of 6:1).

When it comes to people on the autism spectrum, however, it's estimated that only around 10% of them are savants, and not all of them with talents deemed worthy of a TV documentary.

So, when I think of those things that gave me information about autism - pamphlets and media coverage through films - none of those things gave me an accurate picture of what autism actually was.
My brother is nothing like Raymond Babbitt in "Rain Man" and that pamphlet was wrong about a lot of things.

~~~

My brother and myself have shared many intimate, heart-felt moments, from playing dinosaurs as children to lots of hugs, moments where we shared genuine laughter, from holding new members of the family in our arms to singing and re-enacting moments from film and television.

I've seen my brother become upset when he heard a voice recording of himself, seen him physically wrestled just to get his haircut, seen him hurt Mam and tussle with Dad, as well as our many fights as youngsters. I've seen him slip and have his lower lip impaled by the sharp edge of a fridge after he copied me in climbing up the kitchen cupboards as a child. I've seen tears of pain in my mother's eyes from bullies pointing and laughing at him right in front of her face and seen local kids gather to mock him at our garden gates. But I've also seen others being kind to him and giving him a "thumbs up".

For you see, as well as being wrong in many ways, that pamphlet did not prepare me for half the fear that came with having an autistic brother. It said nothing about the worries I'd have for the future - Who will look after him when I'm gone? What if I carry the 'Autistic Gene', if there is one? What if he lashes out at Mam when Dad or I aren't around? What if the bullies catch him alone?

Because of the lack of accurate information about autism as well as the underfunded and poor support generally available to families like mine, I decided to write my own 'guide' to having an autistic brother -

"Brawd Autistico" ('brawd' being the Welsh word for 'brother').

It is my witness statement - a full account of what life is really like with an autistic sibling. The main aim of my blog is simply to educate people on the realities of autism, as well as put to rest a few myths.

For the future of all individuals and families with autism, my brother and I have a lot to say.

Parents and families have so much to share.

It's time we said it.

~~~***~~~

Palette *by Susan*

Susan is a mother to 2 adult sons with autism. She works as a counsellor. Her metaphorical fairy-tale is the outcome of years of struggling to navigate the health and educational systems for her sons.

Once upon a time in a land not too far away there was a beautiful garden. It was the most wondrous place. The grasses and ferns and leaves were brighter than words can describe and the blooms were the finest ever seen.

In this garden was every shade and colour, reflecting the myriad palettes of a thousand artists. Here were showers of snowdrops and tiny cream lilies on slender stalks, deep clusters of bluebells and dancing daffodils. Age-old tulips of striking colours, poppies and daisies and cornflowers. Later, lawns and paths would be bathed in blossoms like sparkling snowflakes. In turn, the scent of lilac and honeysuckle and magnolia would overwhelm.

Next the kaleidoscope would begin, of lavender, mauve, turquoise, lime, crimson, carmine, ruby, salmon, apricot, magenta, velvet blue…. all the colours of the rainbow and every imaginable colour as yet unnamed. The sky overarching the garden changed through cream and pink and purple and orange and blue.

Magically the colours merged and drifted and made way for darkness. Then a glittering of brilliant silver stars would appear almost within reach. Spider webs and paler plants would glow in the stillness of the flower beds and borders as the moon followed her path seeing all. Everything in this garden was mysterious and utterly perfect.

In a quiet corner of this garden lived Mercurio, the nurseryman. His talent for producing an abundance of the finest and most exotic botanical specimens was well known. He was passionate about his work and always found ways to encourage his plants. His energy was unfailing as was his wisdom. He had a vast area of glass houses and potting sheds because the garden was monumental in size and appeared to spread as far as the eye could see. He lived very happily here growing flowers with names like magic – aster, anemone, astilbe, aquilegia, agapanthus, salvia, snapdragon, sweetpea.

Mercurio spent his days and nights cataloguing, potting up, watering the seeds and feeding the shoots. Time seemed to fly by for him, among his watering cans and heaters and fans and plant potions. Sometimes he could be heard talking very quietly to his precious plants - he loved them all.

For company he had a silky black cat that had simply appeared one day. She had silently wandered into his potting shed and found a seat by the window which was always bathed in sunshine. Mercurio had always thought cats to be fickle creatures even though he liked them, nonetheless. She proved to be such a faithful companion he named her Constantia.

Mercurio was always filled with excitement when the new seedlings struggled into the light. He prepared everything to give them the best chance and this year he was especially proud. He was delighted with the shapes of the leaves and the strength of the stems and the emerging colours as the warm sunshine loosened their tight buds.

Out of his entire crop there were always one or two he would give a particular plant food or special soil or whatever extras they needed. Slowly and surely each one would grow into its own unique self - some tall, others short, some showy and bright and their companion's pastel and shy. He cherished them all for their differences and variety.

They soon outgrew their little pots and he planted them alongside their companions. The temperature of the nursery was carefully controlled but sometimes, if there was a small sudden chill, a few of the plants would shiver; if it became unexpectedly warm they would wilt ever so slightly.

Constantia the cat seemed to know when a particular plant was struggling and she would walk over and sniff it with her cool nose, oh so delicately. Then she would curl up beside it for hours and snooze and purr as only cats know how, sometimes opening one eye out of curiosity and then silently closing it again.

As time passed, the plants would recover because of this space and time and care. Mercurio always knew some of his plants were more sensitive to their environment but they still grew and flourished if he was helpful, patient and kind.

As they grew, their colours and markings became beautiful and individual and he knew they would bring a singular depth and clarity to the garden. He continued to talk to them and they seemed to nod and smile in the sun.

Life continued happily until one day the Head Gardener arrived. He told Mercurio it was time for all the plants to be moved into the borders in the garden.

"They are all big and strong enough now," he said.

Mercurio had known deep down this time would come but when he thought of some of his plants his heart sank.

"These ones are a bit delicate, and I feel they are not ready. I think we should be patient and give them a little longer," he said.

"Not possible. They will miss their optimum time to take root and bloom. Get them planted out in the main border today," barked the Head Gardener.

Mercurio was bereft but felt he had no choice. He packed all the larger plants up very carefully in his giant wheelbarrow and worked all through the afternoon to set each one safely into its own little patch. It was a lovely evening, still and warm by the time he returned for the remaining plants.

There was a slight breeze as the little plants bounced gently along gravel paths and cobbled walkways until, there in front, lay the grand, wide expanse of the central border. There were blowsy beautiful bushes at the back of the border to give height and background and shelter. In front of the bushes stood the tall flower stems with buds and brilliant petals, revealing the glorious colours that would soon emerge. In front of these came the slightly shorter plants, with jewel-like hanging bells, others with shimmery domes. In the front row there was space for his remaining plants.

Mercurio began to set the plants in straight rows as he had been instructed.

'Oh dear. They look like sentries. This is not a look that suits them,' he thought wistfully.

Constantia stood very close to him in agreement, her oval green eyes enlarging into liquid pools. Mercurio admired the colour of the smallest plant in particular, a warm purple - delicate yet resonant.

Occasionally he gave his plants names and this one became Sugar Plum. He stayed a while and gave all the plants a drink until the sun began to set.

Every day Mercurio continued to work in the big garden. He noticed sadly how Sugar Plum was not thriving, was becoming overcrowded by the surrounding plants. He gently moved the vegetation so Sugar Plum could breathe and spread. Being slower meant being shorter so he gently pushed the taller plants aside to let the warm sunshine in. He gave the plants all they needed and more. The Head Gardener was also very satisfied because all he wanted was a well-maintained garden.

All the plants thrived over the next few weeks though some did better than others. By now there were waxy roses with lush leaves and sharp needle-like thorns climbing slim pagodas. There were compact roses of the brightest hues sending out rambling brambling thorny suckers. The hollyhocks had shot like shooting stars to dizzy heights along with delphiniums of cobalt blue and lupins and foxgloves. A garden in full flower has to be tamed and trimmed and this privilege fell to Mercurio.

Although everything in the garden was good he had a sense of foreboding. Even Constantia appeared troubled and was never far from his side. Everything came to a head a few days later.

The temperature rose sharply and the air was dry with a breeze that rustled ominously. Mercurio and Constantia both startled as thunder crashed and lightning flashed and the rain roared down in torrents. Mercurio thought at least it will cool now and give the plants a chance to recover. Constantia wore a very worried frown.

Once the storm had subsided, Mercurio and Constantia picked their way through broken branches, twigs and debris until they reached the big garden. The Head Gardener was already there surveying the damage and called out when he saw them.

"Work along the garden and do what you can and pull up these damaged plants," he shouted.

Mercurio did not hear this. His beautiful plants lay drowning in the wet, trampled by the force of the storm. Constantia walked around in thoughtful circles nearby. When he had done what he could he rescued the plants. He laid them carefully on his work table to survey the damage. Sugar Plum was looking limp. Constantia increased her circles.

The Master and the cat lived very quietly but they shared an understanding. Few words were passed from man to cat. Mercurio knew the storm had frightened her.

"Don't worry. We needed the rain to soak the earth and cool the air. Everything is in balance again. We need to satisfy all the different areas and species in the garden. All will be well."

Constantia knew that Mercurio was heartbroken as he gazed at Sugar Plum. She walked very near to him and rubbed her nose over his boots as she remembered the day he had planted Sugar Plum in the big border.

"I had to do it Constantia. We had to try," said Mercurio.

The cat felt his sorrow and his feelings of responsibility as she had earlier sensed his dilemma and loneliness about how best to provide all that Sugar Plum needed.

"Now that I understand I will find a better place for Sugar Plum," he said, suddenly brightening.

~~~

After a few days Sugar Plum began to recover in the special container Mercurio had made. He had searched through his stakes and canes and fashioned a support out of willow and this had helped the plant to recover and remain upright. Shades of pink and purple were showing through. Mercurio thought he saw a fleck or two of ochre or perhaps gold.

As time passed Sugar Plum grew into a fine plant which Mercurio felt would add wonderful colour to the garden. One day he saw a small space had appeared in a sheltered sunny part of his favourite flower bed. Sometimes spaces like this appeared and Mercurio often laughed to imagine the plants moving around when he was not looking. He knew immediately this was the place.

Sugar Plum grew into the space and provided colour and pollen for the butterflies and bees. The nearby plants were fine and fairylike and let her take her place. The plant behind Sugar Plum had put out wonderful trumpets which overflowed with rainwater sending cooling drops all around.

By now most of the garden was established and new jewel-like colours came to the eye, of carnelian and jade and lapis. The Head Gardener was astounded by the beauty and suddenly pointed to Sugar Plum.

"This plant is most attractive and surprising and suits this area perfectly. It provides splendid light and colour and is essential to the overall plan. The colour is quite luminous and the markings are quite remarkably iridescent," he said.

Mercurio stood very tall as he replied.

"All these plants are unique and together they make a garden. But I have learned they all have different needs and we have to give them space and time. Although they are all equal and can thrive we must observe each carefully and provide the right conditions. This will unlock their full potential and the future will be limitless. They all have their part to play which we cannot predict or measure. This is how it must be."

The cat nestled up to Mercurio and meowed very loudly. The Head Gardener looked at them both and for the first time he heard and understood.

~~~**~~~

Glossary

for the Untold Stories

(Definitions sourced online)

ADHD: Attention Deficit Hyperactivity Disorder. A condition that is lifelong and can cause problems with behaviour, such as overactivity, restlessness, difficulties in concentrating and organisation. Some people benefit from medication following a diagnosis.

Batman: A superhero that first appeared in comic books by DC comics in 1939. Batman is the alias of Bruce Wayne, a wealthy American living in the imaginary Gotham City. After the murder of his parents, Wayne swears vengeance on criminals and begins his own quest of clearing Gotham City of ill-doers, without revealing his identity. The character has become hugely popular as a superhero over the years, with a vast array of comics, films, TV programmes and merchandise available.

Bret Easton Ellis (born 1964): An American author, screenwriter and director. "Less than Zero" was his debut novel in 1985 and follows the life of Clay, a young college student experiencing the party scene in Los Angeles in 1984.

Chekhov: Anton Chekhov (1860-1904) was a Russian playwright and short story writer, who is considered to be one of the greatest writers of all time. His works continue to be adapted for theatre and screen, such as "Uncle Vanya", "Three Sisters" and "The Cherry Orchard".

Chronic Fatigue Syndrome (CFS): Sometimes referred to as ME, or Myalgic Encephalomyelitis, it can affect anyone but is most common in ages 20-40. Common symptoms are feeling very tired all the time, taking a long time to recover after any physical activity, sleep problems and difficulty in focusing and concentrating. Some people can also have physical problems such as muscle pain, headaches and flu-like symptoms. Treatments include psychological therapy and medicine to manage physical symptoms. This condition is thought to be caused by chronic stress.

Dark Knight Returns: A film released in two parts, in 2012 and 2013, based on Batman's return to clear Gotham City in 1986. His identity is revealed to the world at the end of Part 2.

Dyslexia: A common condition that causes difficulties with reading, spelling and writing. It's a lifelong problem, intelligence isn't affected. There is no treatment as such, but assessments are available and support or aids are given in schools or work places if someone has a diagnosis of dyslexia.

Dyspraxia: Sometimes referred to as Development Co-ordination Disorder (DCD). A lifelong condition that affects physical (motor) co-ordination and movements. Does not affect intelligence and can cause difficulties in tasks that require balance, in learning and sequencing new skills or with hand or body co-ordination. Occupational and Physiotherapists can provide interventions that can help.

Endometriosis: A condition that can affect women of any age, where tissue grows in the reproductive system, such as in the ovaries or womb. It can cause stomach and period pain, nausea and toileting problems, and can prevent women getting pregnant. There is currently no cure, but treatment is by medication and/or surgery.

Fibromyalgia: A long-term condition that causes pain all over the body. It can also cause problems with sleeping, muscle stiffness, problems in concentration or memory and headaches. The cause is unknown but research suggests it can be triggered by stress and treatment is usually a combination of lifestyle changes and psychological support such as CBT (Cognitive Behavioural Therapy).

Francine Prose (born 1947): An American novelist, critic and professor of literature. "Reading like a writer: A guide for people who love books and for those who want to write them" is her book published in 2012, in which she shares her experiences of learning to write and in developing characters and dialogue.

Genetic Testing: A test to identify any genetic differences or susceptibility to certain diseases.

George Bernard Shaw (1856-1950): an Irish playwright, political activist and critic who had a huge impact on Western thinking, culture and politics.

Hangry: A modern term which means someone is bad tempered or irritable as a result of being hungry.

Irritable Bowel Syndrome (IBS): A condition that affects the gastric system, it can cause symptoms such as stomach bloating, discomfort or pain, as well as problems with constipation and/or diarrhoea. It is suggested that it can be caused by stress. IBS is treated with medication and managing a nutritious diet.

Jane Eyre: A novel written by the British author Charlotte Bronte (1816-1855). Published in 1847, the book is regarded as one of the most important romance novels ever written, with its social and religious commentary. It's regularly included on the reading and examination lists of literature courses in schools and universities.

Jessica McCabe: An American actress, writer and YouTube personality. She is the host of a YouTube channel, "How to ADHD".

LGBTQ: An acronym that is used to describe a diverse range of sexualities and gender identities: Lesbian, Gay, Bisexual, Transgender, Queer or Questioning. Sometimes a "plus" or + sign is added to include others, such as pansexuality, and to represent the huge diversity in people.

Man of Steel: A 2013 film based on the Superman character and his attempts to prevent the destruction of humanity.

Neurodivergence: A term for when someone's brain might process, learn or behave differently from what is seen as "typical".

Obsessive Compulsive Disorder (OCD): A mental health condition, characterised by high levels of anxiety. The person can have obsessive thoughts and compulsive behaviours and often worry about bad things happening to them or others. It can have a huge impact on someone's life. The recommended treatments are talking therapies and/or medication.

Power Rangers: An American entertainment programme and merchandise franchise based on a team of teenagers with superhero powers.

Premenstrual Dysphoric Disorder (PMDD): A very severe form of premenstrual syndrome that causes a range of emotional and physical symptoms each month in women. Experiencing PMDD can make it difficult to work, socialise and have healthy relationships. In some cases, it can also lead to suicidal thoughts. Treatments include medication and psychological therapy.

PTSD: Post Traumatic Stress Disorder is an anxiety disorder that can be caused by very stressful or frightening events. People can experience flashbacks of the traumatic event, experience nightmares and insomnia and suffer from low mood, isolation and guilt. It is treated with anti-depressant medication and/or psychological input.

Sensory Processing: The way the body receives, organises and interprets information from our senses. In order for us to understand the world around us, the body processes information from all of our senses, including sight, touch, smell and taste. Some people can have a Sensory Processing Disorder, which means that their brain has difficulties with this sensory processing mechanism in some way.

Superman: A superhero produced by DC Comics in 1938, who has remained popular. The character is based on the story of a baby born on the fictional planet Krypton and sent to earth by his parents. He is found and subsequently raised by farmers and named Clark Kent; over time he develops superhero powers such as incredible strength and impervious skin and uses these abilities to fight crime. Superman is the archetype of a superhero – he wears a bright, caped costume and changes from his alias of journalist Clark Kent when he needs to fight the baddies!

Synaesthesia: A neurological condition in which information meant to stimulate one of your senses stimulates several of them. For example, hearing music might enable some people to hear it but also see it as colours or shapes.

Section 3

Your Story

Y ou've read about the story of autism.

You've read stories that have finally been brought into the world from people on the autism spectrum along with those affected by it in some way or another. And now we have arrived at Your Story.

But why is your story important? If you do not have autism or do not know anyone with a diagnosis, you would be forgiven for being unsure as to the relevance of your story, but here's the thing; you/we/us, we are all part of the autism story too.

In order for us to understand why the world is such a challenging place for people on the spectrum, we have to look at ourselves and this means considering our own stories. What these are and how they may contribute to the challenges faced by those with autism.

So, let's think about you.

~~~

When you were a newborn, entering this beautiful planet of ours, taking your first gasps of life-giving oxygen and opening your eyes to the world around you ... did you worry about what the doctor thought of you? Were you concerned about the dimples in your thighs? Were you paralysed with fear that your parents would think you weren't good enough for them?

Of course not.

You screamed "I'M HERE!" to announce your beautiful existence and then you went on to demand fluid and warmth and love in that same voice, without bothering about how big your nose was and whether your nappies were the right style for the season.

So, when did all the anxiety and worry about 'stuff' start? You know the 'stuff' I mean ...

 .... those ideas of not being good enough,
 .....of worrying what your neighbours and friends think about you
 .....of feeling that you can't cope
 .....you can't succeed
 .....you're not clever enough
 .....not rich enough
 .....you don't have the perfect body ...

Well, the truth is that you grew those.

They weren't there at the beginning when you were born. You grew them from your life experiences – from the people around you, the events that shaped you and the things that scared you.

Essentially, you made up stories about the world.

Let's consider an example here. A young child who is startled by the loud barking of a neighbour's dog could potentially grow up with a fear of dogs. That makes perfect sense from a survival point of view. Small child versus large, loud dog. But it no longer makes sense when you are 50 years old and avoiding going out of the house because next door's terrier is in the garden.

Reflect on some of your fears – we all have them.

If you think back to when you first experienced it you can usually make a link to a specific event. Undoubtedly this event will be at the root of your fear. Remember, children are sponges – they pick up everything around them and create their own stories about the world – including those based on fear.

Another example may be your parents working very long hours in manual jobs. From this you might believe that in order to be a successful adult you must work long hours in a job which is physically demanding. You might construct a narrative that a desk or creative job is simply not as important.

You see, unknowingly, we pick up all sorts of stories throughout our lives – most of them without conscious realisation. Some stories may be smaller; a home isn't a home without a cat in it; we always have fish on a Friday; we never wear shoes in the house; or you might have certain family rituals for birthdays or Christmas.

Some stories are significantly larger; they could be around your religion; your thoughts about life and what happens after death; the expectations you have of a partner. Every single person's collection of stories is unique to them. No one single person is the same and every individual will have hundreds, if not thousands of these stories.

Think again about yours. About your stories large and small, about the rituals and habits you may have adopted from childhood and your thoughts around these. Also, stories are often hidden. It isn't until we shine a spotlight that we recognise what they are and how they impact us. And they can be deep, really deep.

Like a sculptor you will have honed and chiselled away at each story to make it suit you and then built beliefs around them until they have become part of who you are. This is how we believe hypnotherapy works – by targeting the subconscious beliefs you have adopted and breaking the negative systems you have created. Talking therapies can't always do this simply because when you verbalise something, you aren't necessarily targeting your deep-seated subconscious beliefs. Hence we don't always find talking therapies to be effective. They can be great for some things but will often not target the stories that you have hidden deep inside your subconscious, built from a lifetime of living on this planet.

And there is one more thing.

Your stories are hugely affected by something else: your sense of survival.

~~~

I think we all appreciate that our brains are an amazing piece of kit. Perfectly formed and developed over thousands of years it is the very thing that keeps us alive. In fact, that's its job. To keep us alive. So, when you are thinking about doing a parachute jump for charity, what might your brain scream at you? Or, if your boss asks you to deliver a lecture in front of a hundred people, what message will your brain send? Or, when you want to move house to an area where you know no one, what emotion will your brain fire up? Or, if it's a challenge to even leave the house, what will your brain be saying?

If, as we know, it is our brains job to keep us alive, then in all likelihood in these and millions of other scenarios, your brain will be telling you not to do any of these things and why. And then it uses its finest tool...

Anxiety.

It flicks the switch of your Autonomic Nervous System and floods you with those uncomfortable physical sensations to persuade you even more that ...

No! You Should Not Do That Thing!

Even when it might be something that is actually very good for you in the long run, your brain will still tell you not to do it, because our brains can't see the long-term future. Our brains live in the moment. They function in the here and now and they absolutely do not like the fact that we want to do something different or trying something new. Why? Because, thinks our brain, we might die - and we just might.

So, the brain tells us not to do that 'dangerous' thing and goes back to its happy, predictable life of sameness, routine and safety.

From a survival standpoint our brains do a great job. They employ those amazing stress responses and utilise all of our mind and body systems to keep us alive and safe. But, as we've just discovered, it also stops us from doing many other things.

People who engage in activities such as extreme sports have learnt to channel this process into excitement and challenge, and to switch off or to ignore the irrational thoughts which try to stop them. Of course, this can sometimes and sadly go too far (if that person doesn't calculate the risks they are taking) but if you let your brain dominate every aspect of your life then you will potentially never leave your comfort zone. Whilst that's not necessarily a bad thing, we know that growth (personal and professional), never happens within our comfort zones so perhaps, if we are not able to step outside of this, we may forever feel unsettled, stuck and fearful.

Going back to our brains and the knowledge that they love sameness, routine and safety – what happens when we come across someone who is not like us? How does our brain react?

What happens if we see someone with a different skin colour, or a person speaking another language, or talking about issues that we don't understand or choosing to love someone of their own sex or wearing clothes in a way we never would? We are all different, but our brain likes sameness, routing and safety so can feel threatened when it comes across something for which it has no road map. It tells us that because we don't understand then we have to be scared because ultimately that's the best way it knows to keep us alive. When we experience this fear it's easier to return to our place of comfort, to our own stories and those we have seen in the media because that's what we know. That's the familiar. That's the known. And it is there we feel comfortable. It's easier to sit with what we believe we know rather than broaden our thinking because if we do that it causes anxiety and as a species we just don't like to feel anxious.

"Cognitive Dissonance" is the name of this process, where we refuse to believe something if it makes us feel anxious and scared, regardless of how true it may be. This explains why it can be hard to win an argument with some people, even when you show them scientific proof and research they can still disagree with you regardless simply because it scares them to consider an alternative explanation. Which comes back to anxiety. You are challenging their beliefs which makes them feel anxious and oddly, we seem to feel more comfortable avoiding anxiety than we do facing an unfamiliar truth.

Isn't that interesting? People literally go around denying things, or making stories up, because they don't want to feel that their long-held assumptions are wrong. We know that if we challenge our assumptions, for many of us it can cause incredible anxiety so we choose to continue with our stories. We feel that it is better to ignore things or believe in untruths rather than allow another viewpoint and let the anxiety in.

This behaviour is why some people have meteoric shifts in life when they are faced with life-altering situations such as a life-threatening illness, or a car crash, or losing someone close to them, or going through some kind of trauma. Stories and assumptions change when these kinds of Big Life Things happen but unless we experience them we can live our lives in a kind of fairytale which keeps us trapped and unhappy.

None of this is wrong though, quite the contrary. All humans do this. We are the sum of hundreds and thousands of years of evolution, and we are also affected by the genes of our ancestors as well as those who came before us. The problem is that living in this way, in a kind of fairytale where we remain in our comfort zone, can cause us to feel anxious and depressed. Why? Because it feels too scary to change anything. But here's the game changer ...

If we can create a story about something, we can un-create it.

We have the power to change so much once we become aware of what is happening. Powerful stuff.

So, I want you to do a little exercise around stories. Look at this list and think about your emotional response to each of the people on it. What is your immediate reaction to each one of these? Don't think about it, just go on your gut feeling.

Ready? Let's go.

-     Skinheads
-     A woman wearing a hijab
-     People with tattoos on their neck and face
-     Drag queens
-     Preachers
-     A drug user
-     People in a same-sex marriage
-     Devout Catholics
-     Someone who is an amputee
-     Non-binary people
-     People who are extremely overweight
-     Very wealthy people
-     People claiming benefits
-     Someone with a stutter
-     Someone with an alcohol problem
-     Someone with 10 children
-     An Orthodox Jewish person
-     Someone with face piercings
-     Someone in a wheelchair
-     Someone with a large birthmark

Did you notice your reaction to each one?

I guarantee your reaction to every person on this list will have been different in some way or another. For some you may not have experienced much of a reaction whereas others may have provoked a significantly stronger response.

Did you feel a fear-based or negative reaction towards any of them?

If you did, that's okay. All it means is that you have developed a story or belief about that particular type of person through your years of learning and growth. Many of these feelings will be unconscious and you won't even be aware that you have them until they surface, but somewhere along the line you will have learnt that reaction from someone/somewhere.

Remember what we said earlier about babies?

A baby wouldn't have any reaction to the people in that list. As long as that person gives them safety, food, love and shelter then a baby doesn't care what colour their skin is or what their life choices are or what clothes they wear. So, we know that when we were born we didn't have these assumptions or stories or pre-conceptions. We learned them, which means we have an emotional connection to it (that varies depending upon its root) and this leads to an associated level of anxiety. This level of anxiety will then increase when we seek to make a change.

~~~

Once we become aware of the way we think about the world and realise that we are all products of our life experiences (and resultant stories) then we can start to make changes.

You might be wondering why I am telling you this and what relevance it has to the subject matter. Simply put, in order for us to begin to understand others, those who are 'different'

170

and those who see the world through an alternate lens, we need to understand through our own stories how *we* see the world. And to realise that everyone else does the same through their own stories. We need to learn to accept that we are ALL different on so many levels, because we are all individuals and every single one of us has a different set of stories.

And it is this that makes us unique.

Can you see that it's not just what we look like that makes us different?

Nor is it the colour of our skin or how tall or heavy we are, or how much money we have in our bank account or which deity we pray to. It's our story-set, and as a result, how we see the world.

If we take it a stage further we can see that this impacts so many areas of our lives - what we do for work, the life partner we choose, whether we have children, the food we buy, the things we spend our money on, how we see ourselves and the risks we are willing to take. Did you know, for example, that of the 46 American Presidents to hold office, 12 of them lost a parent when they were a child? That's almost a third. Equally, 67% of British Prime Ministers (from the beginning of the 19th Century to World War II), lost a parent before the age of 16. Is this a coincidence?

Not according to author Malcolm Gladwell who calls this "Eminent Orphans" and points out that the death of a mother or father can be a propellant which 'sends people catapulting into life'. In other words, because these children are on their own and because a terrible thing has already happened to them, their story becomes one of persistence, invention and of charting their own way without worrying about what might happen. Survival becomes about taking chances, and not worrying so much about the outcome.

That's their story.

Of course, we can't say for sure that such trauma in early life makes us more successful. There are people whose experiences will cause mental health problems and those who will make unhelpful life choices, but in many research studies there is a theme of "eminent orphans" doing very well in life.

It's also worth bearing in mind that usually, children with loving families who get protection and support, also flourish in terms of their physical and mental health as well as their overall life enrichment. It is also true that children with missing parents generally develop extra resilience and grit and self-reliance in life – which are also ingredients for societal success.

This can show us that it is not WHAT happens to us but rather how we THINK about it and what we subsequently DO that makes the difference. This is the STORY we have created.

Consider those inspirational quotes we see online. Pictures of rainbows which say things like, "It's not what happens to you, but how you react to it that matters," or, "What people say to you is their problem; how you respond is yours".

Or the spiritual speaker and author Wayne Dyer who said, "How people treat you is their karma; how you react is yours."

Given what we have discovered and learned via this book and its untold stories, regardless of what you think about inspirational quotes, we can see that these 'truths' are not far off the mark. The fact that we are all different on so many levels is a beautiful thing. It's not wrong to be different. If we're trying to 'fit in' with anyone or anything then we are wasting our time because everyone else is doing exactly the same.

Teenagers spend much of their time trying to 'fit in' because they are searching for an identity and someone to connect with, which is an important life process, but if they take it too far they can lose themselves. They will lose their own uniqueness.

It's the same for everyone. We try to make changes to reduce our anxiety but we are basing these changes on our perception of not 'fitting in' and as opposed to reality. Remember, in our world, everyone else is doing exactly the same thing.

We are all trying to 'fit in' – with what? – and it is ultimately making us ill. We need to realise that it is in our very differences we will find health, happiness and societal success. It is possible to have social connection (important for our sense of well-being) and meaningful relationships (crucial for joy and mental health) and still be our own unique selves.
We don't need to own a certain brand of trainers to be loved. This is a made-up story – one from which sports companies make a huge profit. Big businesses understand how to manipulate our fears and anxieties and then provide us with the solution – a way of 'belonging' – for a short time at least.

Industries such as the beauty industry depend on men and women feeling bad about themselves after all, who would buy their products if they were perfectly happy with how they looked?

That's why these big companies employ psychologists, and why advertisements are slanted to sell that very thing which will 'make us happy'. This message can be at odds with the reality of (say in the case of fast food, alcohol and carbonated drinks) over consumption, and the resultant damage to our health and wellbeing that can be caused. The very thing we are being encouraged to buy so that we 'fit in' and are 'happy' can also have a huge detrimental effect on us.

So perhaps it's time to consider how much more of our money we are going to spend on material items which do not ultimately bring us joy. Maybe we should start thinking about the things that our brains are preventing us from doing – taking that amazing holiday or trip or staying small – because it is in charge and tells us not to. Is it possible to give ourselves the freedom to simply be US?

Life has endless possibilities if we can just be brave enough to embrace them. To erase those old stories and write new ones. You don't need to find answers right now, you just need to be open to the possibilities. And if you are, you might find yourself writing a new story.

One that could change your life and may just change your world.

~~~

Difference, bizarrely, is what gives us unity and enables us to love each other and to work together to solve problems. It is also what gives us the best chance of survival. Although our brains are only wanting to keep us safe, they are also doing us a huge disservice by preventing us from understanding how positive 'differences' can be. We may feel anxious but diversity is the key and this is what will help us to do great things, regardless of the learned messages we are receiving from our brain.

We need to know that it's okay to feel uncomfortable and anxious at times – it's natural, it's temporary and it passes very quickly for most people. And once you become aware of and understand this, that's when things begin to change. You will develop the skill to be an observer of your own thoughts - instead of simply a follower.

Watch and listen to how your brain reacts next time you think about doing something a little differently or taking a leap into the unknown. Maybe you'll be thinking about writing that book, or asking someone out on a date, or applying for a new job. Watch how your anxiety and those irrational thoughts kick in - and now you will understand what your brain is doing.

Try it – think about something new that challenges you a little, it doesn't need to be anything big. Does it cause those flutters of anxiety?

Listen. What is your brain trying to tell you? What message is it sending with those flutters of anxiety? Is it telling you to stop doing this thing?

Watch and listen and you will see how your stories have been created.

~~~

Not all brains are the same.

There are people whose brains are structured differently or they process information differently or work in a slightly contrary way. These people are exactly the same as everyone else, the only difference is in the way that they think – which is dictated to by the differences in their brain.

Neurological and mental health specialities are growing all the time in their understanding and knowledge of the massively complex human brain, and we are constantly discovering new and exciting information about it through innovative research. Bringing it back to autism though, there is still so much that we don't know and we are continuing to actively research why some children develop this condition and others do not.

It's not just people with autism who are different though. Hopefully, from the information provided here, you can see that we are all different. We are different because of the unique stories we have weaved about the world. We are different in our life experiences and what we have made of them - but one thing that we do all have in common ... we all fear being different and we are all scared of it.

Of course, this is an evolutionary survival strategy in many ways – if you didn't fit in with your caveman club, then you would be turned out. Probably to a tragic end of starvation or death by sabre tooth tiger, so it's in your interest to fit in with the crowd. But thousands of years later we are still building our sense of self and identities on the people around us. It really matters to us what people think. A passing comment or a lack of "likes" on social media, for example, can really ruin your day. And to feel as if we not only fit in, but are truly winning at life, we have to develop some pretty advanced social strategies – saying the right things at the right times, looking a certain way to be accepted, behaving in socially acceptable ways, perhaps not saying what we really want to and being who we really are.

In fact, one of the biggest problems that people with autism have told me they have, is the fear they are different and that they don't "fit in". They will often do all sorts of things to avoid 'being different' and spend a lifetime trying to fit into a world where everyone else is doing exactly the same. We all try to fit in with the newest gadgets, or with the cars we drive, or in the exercise we do, or the clubs we go to, or the jobs we work in, or the shows we watch, or the clothes we wear.

But I think it's crucial to ask, do any of those things make us happy? Really happy?

Over the years, there have been many social movements of rebellion. The punk era is an example of railing against what society expects of you, and some of these movements have led to big social and political changes. They have also sought to show us how important it is to be our authentic selves in order to keep us mentally and physically well. Should we compromise on that in order to fit in?

Ask yourself:

   - How much does social pressure and your need to fit in really impact you?
   - Can you honestly say you are your authentic self at every moment of the day?
   -Do you find yourself sacrificing what you want so that other people are looked after?
   -Do you carry a certain sense of resentment that you can't really say what you want for fear of ridicule or others not liking you?

176

- Do you live a life that is centred around the things that are expected of you, not the things you would want to do?
- If you could be anything, say anything, do anything without fear, what would you be doing?

Imagine what your life could look like if you could just, "Do You".

Wider still than our feelings of inferiority or fear, of trying to fit in, are all the ways in which society limits us too.

Think:

- As a man, what stories were you told about how to be?
- As a woman can you wear what you want to? Can you walk down a street at midnight and feel safe?

We have more money, more home comforts and more possessions than we have ever had yet we seem to be sadder than ever. Disconnected. Isolated. With a deep inner knowing that something isn't right. And by trying to maintain this superficiality, of being something we are not, we have effectively isolated those who we believe to be different. We have stereotyped and scorned people who might look different, move differently, see things differently so that we can feel safe and belong – but has that simply isolated us as a society?

If we can begin to understand why these things have happened, we can challenge how we see things, change our stories and see our lives change too.

Though today, some cultural and societal practices of division and discrimination persist, these age-old ideas of difference are being challenged and we are entering a new dawn of understanding, unity and unification. Why? Because we are finally beginning to understand the price we are paying for trying to fit into a place we were never meant to fit.

This price can mean catastrophic levels of mental and physical health problems.

We need to understand how important it is to honour our own authenticity. And that has been driven home to me more than ever in my work with those on the autistic spectrum. We need to embrace who we are and we don't need to 'fit in', we really don't.

And when we realise that, that's when everything will change for us – and for everyone.

The truth is, once we start to examine our own minds – examine why we think in the way that we do and the stories we have created, how society has conditioned us in many ways to seek those things that don't bring us joy - that's when we start to see the beauty in diversity and WE all thrive.

We are no longer threatened by "difference" or feel scared of someone who might look or think or behave in a different way. And when we get to this point, then we can engage and include and connect with each other for the sake of our own communities and wider world.

Then we will have true neuro-unity.

Section 4
Going From Here

And so we have arrived at the final part of the book, and the last leg of our story together.

We've seen and understood the autism story and why we are where we are in our comprehension of neurodiversity along with the impact it has had on generations of people.

We've read the words and listened to the voices in the untold stories – real lives and real people - and you've read about your story – why you think in the way that you do, where your values and beliefs come from, and why it can be hard for our brains to cope with and accept difference.

Where the story goes now is really up to you.

We can carry on as we always have – after all, there is comfort in familiarity and the way we've previously done things – but the problem is, we are still lacking solutions to huge global issues. We continue to battle discrimination on many different levels and we are facing worldwide mental health epidemics and rising suicide levels in our young people.

For me personally, I think we need a new strategy, and we need different kinds of minds to tackle the problems we face. To do that, we must recognise and alter the way we all think.

I genuinely hope that what you have read so far has launched you onto the first steps of your own journey.

The remaining chapters in *Part 4* will now focus on the more practical things you can do. There are suggested steps and strategies to recognise and support people on the spectrum and the wider neurodivergent community. Some of this information is aimed at professionals – teachers and educators, health and social care staff, criminal justice and emergency staff - key people who are vital in recognising and supporting the people they serve. But some of it is aimed at everyone.

There is also more information on what you can expect in a diagnostic assessment and a list of support services and further resources you may wish to explore.

And don't forget, the autistic people I know and work with have given me their top ten tips for living with autism – advice that they (and us) need to hear when things get tough. These can be found in *Chapter 3* of this section and is a great list to keep to hand.

Chapter 1

Being Assessed for Autism - What to Expect

Some people choose not to have a formal assessment for a diagnosis of autism and prefer to self-identify; it's your decision whether you want to be referred for a formal diagnostic assessment. There are checklists and brief assessments that you can do online but remember that these are only a general guide and can't replace a thorough clinical assessment.

Commonly, the AQ-10 (Autism Quotient) test is used to screen adults for traits of autism. It's a set of 10 questions which highlights if someone could have signs of autism. Your GP might fill this in with you before sending a referral for an assessment.

NHS Assessments

Diagnostic assessments for autism are generally provided free of charge by the NHS and usually require a referral from your GP practice. Because different areas of the United Kingdom have differing commissioning and funding arrangements, the length of time that you will have to wait for an assessment will vary from place to place. On being referred you will receive an acknowledgement letter which should advise you of the current wait time.

Each area and Trust will also have different service arrangements but generally, children under 18 years of age will be seen by a CAMHS (Child and Adolescent Mental Health Service) or a Neurodevelopment Team. Sometimes referrals for children are made by educational psychologists or teachers - with parental consent. Children and adults with Learning Disabilities are usually assessed by their community Learning Disability team. Adults will be seen by a different team – most areas are developing autism specific diagnostic teams for adults; these are generally for those aged 18 years and above.

Some assessments are sub-contracted – that is, a private company is commissioned by the NHS to provide the diagnostic assessments and where you will be seen varies from service to service. Some offer face to face sessions – either at health centres or offices, or sometimes in your own home - others are virtual only so you will be assessed via an internet link.

Most diagnostic teams are made up of different professionals – a multi-disciplinary team. Again, this will vary from service to service but generally the teams include Psychologists, Occupational Therapists, Speech and Language Therapists, Specialist Nurses and sometimes Social Workers. Some teams will also have a Consultant/Doctor. All staff in these teams will have to be trained to use the specialist standardised assessment tools to assess for autism.

The NHS have guidelines on how assessment teams should be practicing and the National Institute for Health and Care Excellence (NICE) is the quality body that develops practice standards and guidelines on how services should be provided. This is based on research which shows what the most effective ways of working are. There are guidelines on what standardised assessments should be used and different services might use different combinations of assessments.

Here are a few of the assessments generally used for both adults and children:

ADOS – Autism Diagnostic Observation Schedule
ADI-R – Autism Diagnostic Interview – Revised
DISCO – Diagnostic Interview for Social & Communication Disorders

There are other tools that can be used specifically for young children or toddlers. More information can be found online and via the National Autistic Society's website:

www.autism.org.uk/advice-and-guidance/topics/diagnosis/
diagnostic-tools/all-audiences

Generally, these tools rely on two things:

1. A description and history of the person's development and difficulties.
2. An observation of the person by asking them questions or engaging them in some basic table-top activities.

The assessment itself can take up to 4 hours. Some services might do this in one appointment or it can be divided over more. Sometimes practitioners might go into a school or nursery to observe a child in the classroom to see how they engage with other children, for example.

There is no medical examination, the assessment is done through asking questions and some basic activities – such as looking at an image or reading a book and commenting on what you/they think is happening. And, as we've previously mentioned, the person being assessed will be asked to take someone along with them who can comment on what they were like as a child. With children, much of the assessment is done through observation and play activities.

After the assessment you will be advised as to what the next step is. Some services will ask to see you again to feedback the result, or they may do this by telephone or virtual appointment. You should then get a full and comprehensive report of the assessment and findings – regardless of whether you/they meet the criteria for a diagnosis. Some services write very comprehensive and detailed reports which include a number of recommendations and suggestions on what support might be needed. These can be extremely helpful. It's important to keep a copy of this report because you/they may need it in the future. This might be, for example, if you/they are asking for support from school or university, or if you/they want to apply for benefits or other support.

It is your/their report and you/they are not legally bound to share it with anyone unless you/they wish to. Your GP will get a copy but after that it's up to you/they who you/they share it with.

If you/they are not happy with the outcome of the assessment you/they can ask for a second opinion.

After the assessment the level of post-diagnostic support you/they receive will depend on what is being funded and offered locally. Sometimes the NHS teams offer post-diagnostic groups or one-to-one support for adults, or you/they may be given information and signposting to charities which might do this in your area. At present there is a lack of post diagnostic support unfortunately, though I understand that increased funding (from local Government) is starting to be allocated to these services.

If the diagnosis was given to a child there may be parent support groups or help available in school. All schools have a SEN (Special Educational Needs) system in place which assesses what support a child would need in school. Children may also need an EHC (Education Health and Care) plan if they require more support than the school currently provides. If you are unsure what is available, do ask the team assessing your child what they are able to offer.

In all situations, don't be afraid to ask questions. The professionals working in these services are well aware that most people are anxious and worried about the assessment and are more than happy to offer support as needed.

Private Assessments

Because NHS waiting times can be lengthy some people opt for a private assessment. These are available for children and adults and range in price in terms of what you get for your money. There are a few considerations to think about before buying a private diagnostic assessment:

- Check that the practitioners are registered with a health body such as the HCPC (Health and Care Professions Council). You can check their register for free at: www.Hcpc-uk.org.
- Ask how they deliver their assessments – face-to-face or virtually - and make sure you are comfortable with this.
- Ask what diagnostic tools they will be using.
- Ensure you know exactly what you are getting for your money – is it just an assessment, a report, or do they offer post-diagnostic support too?
- Check that your local services – such as school or NHS – will accept a private diagnosis. I have heard of some services which don't offer support because the diagnosis was given outside of their organisation.

Receiving a Diagnosis

Getting, or not getting a diagnosis can be a very emotional and stressful time. For many people it's a positive thing, but it can also feel overwhelming. Some people take a long time to reflect and adjust whilst others adapt fairly quickly. If you do receive a diagnosis don't expect to feel better overnight. Set yourself a realistic target for adjustment.

It is important to make sure that support is available to talk about your/ their diagnosis and what this might mean. This could come in the form of family or friends, but equally you/they can ask local services for support. If you are a parent with a diagnosed child who is at school ask for their support. You/they can also contact the Local Authority to find out if there are any local charities and support groups which may be able to help.

Often, parents with children who receive an autism diagnosis can experience many difficult and conflicting feelings. As a parent you may feel guilty about something you think you could have done or not done. You may feel sad that your child is "different" in some way or that they need extra support. You might even wonder if you have similar difficulties and could it be that you are on the spectrum too? As well as yourself, it's perfectly normal to have concerns about the impact of your child's diagnosis on the wider family. Regardless, all of these feelings are normal and you will not be the first person to experience these. It's amazing how families and the individuals in them adapt and cope as long as they are provided with the right information and the right support.

Sometimes there are benefits to joining local groups or online forums because it can help to connect with other parents or people on the spectrum. I would suggest double checking that these forums are supportive though because the last thing you/they want is more stress and upset than you are already experiencing.

The key is not to struggle alone. Autism is not a rare condition and there are many people in similar situations.

You just need to find them.

Chapter 2

Tips for Professional and Support Staff

As I've previously mentioned, good autism training is sadly lacking and has been for many years so don't worry if you feel under prepared as a professional or member of support. There are many brilliant resources available online and I have seen training courses being commissioned so I hope that things are changing. The main thing I would advise though is to be open minded. Make sure you listen to your patient/person and tailor any support you offer appropriately.

Each profession will see a different range of people affected by autism. The support a police officer needs to give for example, will be significantly different to that of a nurse or teacher. You will almost certainly encounter someone with autism in your working life and role so it is worth bearing in mind that some of these people may not have an official diagnosis, and that will change how you communicate with and support each individual.

I hope the information and stories in this book have tested your assumptions about what autism looks like, particularly perhaps, as it presents in females.

If you are working with children or young people then you will be key in recognising a child who is experiencing some challenges and will need to proactively explore any difficulties they may present with. Please try not to shy away from having sensitive conversations if you believe someone may have autism. There are so many people who have told me that if it wasn't for their teacher/social worker/counsellor, they would never have known about autism let alone received their diagnosis.

If you suspect that someone might be showing traits of autism, please do act if it's appropriate to do so. Have a conversation with your clinical lead or line manager or staff team and if everyone agrees, have those sensitive conversations with parents or adults.

It is not a waste of time to have an autism assessment, far from it. Even if someone does not get a formal diagnosis, assessments can help to pick up on other problems such as speech and language issues, mental health co-morbidities, or sometimes other conditions such as ADHD or dyspraxia.

Reasonable Adjustments

All public health bodies are expected to make Reasonable Adjustments for people with autism. This is a legal expectation due to autism being classified as a disability under the *Equality Act 2010* - previously the *Disability Discrimination Act*. The key word here is "reasonable".

Adjustments can be small, maybe only minor tweaks to a practice that can really make a difference. Generally, there are two main things to remember when it comes to reasonable adjustments. The goal is to:

1. Reduce anxiety (of the person affected).
2. Increase predictability (of their situation and events).

If you are in a situation where you need to consider making reasonable adjustments think about the ways you could do that in your workplace or at home. Remember though - one size does not fit all, and adjustments have to be made with each individual in mind.

If you're not sure, ask the person or their caregiver what you can do to support them whilst they are in school, or work, or in hospital.

Examples of Reasonable Adjustments

These are examples and suggestions of adjustments. I'm sure you can think of many more potential ones that you can make, depending on what each person needs.

Communication:
- Ask someone how they prefer to communicate – some people don't like using the telephone, for example. Think about offering a variety of ways that someone could communicate with you, such as text or email.
- Not expecting or encouraging someone to look directly at you if they struggle to do so.
- Avoiding complex instructions or lots of complicated information giving – break things down into chunks.
- Be literal and clear in what you are saying, don't assume people understand.
- Without being patronising you can ask someone to repeat what they've understood from what you have said.
- Give plenty of processing time and don't expect immediate answers to questions.
- Keep your communication to the point.
- Make sure environmental distractions are minimised, especially if giving new or complex information.
- Use visual cues or supporting booklets or sheets to support what you're saying.
- Be very clear about the purpose of what you are doing and what might happen next and give the person plenty of opportunity to ask questions.

Arranging Support and Interventions:
- If you are a professional and visiting someone or seeing them in a clinic, offer a choice of appointments and times.
- When meeting face to face, find out where the individual would prefer to meet.

- Think about where you see people – what is the environment like? Would someone be comfortable to sit in the waiting room or school cafeteria, for example. Think about the lighting and the sounds and the proximity of other people.
- If you are working with adults, tell that person they can bring someone with them to an appointment for support if they wish.
- Ask if the person has a 'communication passport' or similar which sets out their communication preferences. These are available online to complete.
- Be very clear about what is going to happen and what happens next. Think about providing visual information and leaflets for people to take away with them.
- Consider where you could provide quiet spaces or places where people can go if they need to.
- Think about the impact of groupwork or study groups.
- Try and maintain consistency in the staff who might see or work with the person. Having to meet a lot of new and unfamiliar people can increase stress.
- Think about the impact of change on somebody and try not to alter arrangements once they are made.
- Always remember to work with someone in their own individual context – work in a person-centred way.
- Involve family members and carers in an appropriate manner to ensure the most effective support.

Aids and Adaptations:
There may be gadgets or equipment or even environmental adjustments that can be helpful, particularly for people with sensory sensitivities. These can be key in preventing overwhelm. You could consider things such as:

- Noise cancelling headphones.
- Sensory toys.
- Provision of quiet or sensory rooms.
- Weighted blankets or comfort items.

- Enabling someone to have a space in a quiet office.
- Self-controlled lighting or heating equipment.
- Self-soothe boxes.
- A quiet place where someone can stim.
- Practical equipment such as screen covers for computers or apps for time management or studying.
- Considering flexible school or work arrangements – this could be arriving and leaving after everyone else or shortening the time spent in class or in the workplace.

There are many websites and online resources with more suggestions on reasonable adjustments. **The National Autistic Society's website** – *www.autism.org* – has lots of information on reasonable adjustments as well as information for employers and educational providers.

There are other resources such as Autism Alert cards, Profile Sheets, Communication Preference Cards and Hospital Passports that can also be used to support people on the spectrum. Not everyone will find these useful as again, adjustments must be appropriate for the person they are designed for.

If you are on the spectrum and are in higher education or employment, there is a legal requirement for your place of work or study to provide you with an assessment to help support you in terms of making appropriate adjustments. Not having adjustments in place means that people on the spectrum, whether a child or an adult, might potentially miss out on treatment and support in education or in the workplace.

As a professional you may also want to consider how you can make your place of work more aware and accepting of neurodiversity. There are a few ways you can do this:

- Think about the training you have received. Is it adequate and is there opportunity for regular refresher training for staff?

- Can you build in Continuing Professional Development activities around knowledge of autism?
- Consider what support you might need from your organisation in terms of making reasonable adjustments.
- You could think about developing a neurodiversity lead role where key staff can lead the team in terms of knowledge of autism, providing expertise and leading on necessary changes. Many places have developed "champion" roles where it has been extremely successful in changing and improving the culture of services.
- Apply for any available funding to develop resources – some may be resources such as self soothe kits or sensory equipment in schools through to ergonomic equipment for the workplace or provision of specialist equipment or learning resources.

As a professional you are key in recognising, understanding and supporting children and adults on the spectrum, and because it is a legal requirement for reasonable adjustments to be made, also think about this:

If people who have significantly changed the world had never had the opportunity to achieve their potential, where would we be? There would be no aeroplanes in the sky, very little scientific understanding and no computers or internet.

Surely we owe it to everyone to reach their potential, regardless of how they see the world.

Chapter 3

Living with Autism

Being autistic can bring a unique set of challenges to daily life and the people I have worked with over the last ten years have identified the difficulties they've faced and how they have coped with them. Getting a diagnosis is only the first step to a whole new journey – one of understanding, dealing with things that can be very stressful or difficult, and of working towards having the life that you desire.

We can't always achieve everything we want. I would love to be an Olympic boxer but realistically even if I train hard, eat all the right foods and get into the most positive mindset, my age might mean that I would struggle to get to the standard required for an Olympic gold medal. But that doesn't mean that I can't still train and enjoy going to the boxing club or have a fit and sporty life.

Equally, having the right mindset and knowing ourselves is important – recognising that there is nothing wrong or "broken" about you because you have autism, yet knowing there are certain situations which might cause you difficulties and having good, effective coping strategies to deal with these when they happen.

Avoiding overwhelm or "meltdown" is extremely important, because not only are these episodes distressing and exhausting, but they can also take a long time to recover from. So, maintaining a lifestyle where you keep your stress levels as low as possible, getting adequate rest or periods of time on your own, eating nutritionally adequate foods and enough fluids to keep you hydrated are all important.

Let's take a look at the Top Ten coping strategies suggested by those I have worked with. These are the things that they, as autistic adults, wish that they had been told at the beginning of their autism story.

They might not be appropriate or realistic for you, but it will help you to consider and reflect on what might work.

Number One: Understand and accept that you are not broken and never were. Society has always struggled to understand autism or any kind of difference. Many of the things that happened to you were due to this, not because there was anything wrong with you. Books like this one will help to make things better. Some people with autism like to get involved in raising the awareness of it through training or speaking or developing their own websites or social media platforms. You don't have to do that of course, but you can let go of feeling worthless or that things were your fault in any way. Because they weren't your fault, and you are simply perfect as you are.

Number Two: Doing what you want to do. Not everyone with autism wants to make friends or get a job or join social clubs, and that's absolutely fine. But if you do want to do those things then think about ways you can do that. Don't let your life pass you by because you are too anxious to try. Find a way of taking small steps towards your goals – even stepping out of the front door or saying "Hi" to someone can be a start. Look for support if you need it and don't be afraid to ask for help.

Number Three: Energy Maintenance. Doing certain things will really sap your energy battery. If you go to school or college or work during the day then you will be mentally and physically drained in the evening so don't plan anything demanding or stressful - that's a sure-fire way to overwhelm. When you are doing activities which take a lot of energy (and that will be different for everyone), make sure you have rest and recovery periods built into your day.

Number Four: Rest and Recovery. Think about what recharges you, what makes you feel rested and relaxed. That could be engaging in the things you really enjoy such as a special interest or listening to music or gaming. Make sure you have time to do this every day. This is really important to prevent overwhelm or meltdown. Also make sure you get plenty of sleep – everyone needs different amounts so think about what works best for you. Using a smart watch or fitness app can show you your sleep patterns.

Number Five: Sensory Stuff. Do you struggle with sensory things such as sounds or lights? What could you do to make those things better? There are some things you can't change (like the music in supermarkets for example – urgh) but you could get a gadget or piece of equipment that might help such as noise-cancelling headphones or filters for your glasses. It can be difficult to know if you have sensory problems when you've had a lifetime of it but an autism assessment can usually pick up on this and you could ask someone you know well what their experiences might be. Sometimes it might be possible to avoid sensory triggers. For example, if you really don't like supermarkets, shop online where possible.

Number Six: Understanding Anxiety. Most people hate feeling anxious, it's uncomfortable and not a pleasant feeling, however, research shows that most people with autism have significant anxiety and have had it from childhood. Researchers don't know why that is but there's a theory that it's because autistic people find it hard to predict the world and what people might do in an intuitive way, so it causes anxiety. What that means essentially is that there's no point trying to get rid of anxiety because it's unlikely to ever go away completely, but what you can do is recognise when you get anxious and then find ways to try and minimise it or recover from it. Utilising tools such as meditation or breathwork apps can be helpful, watching relaxing videos on YouTube, engaging in sports or enjoyable activities, using gadgets or sensory equipment and distracting yourself can all help to bring your stress levels down. Exercise and moving your body (even if it's just a walk in the park or the garden) is really good at balancing out brain chemicals and making us feel better. Doing this will also prevent you developing more significant mental and physical health problems.

Number Seven: Using technology. There are some useful apps and resources online which can be helpful. Some are apps that can help you manage your work or school life as well as apps such as *Brain in Hand* that can help you navigate your day.

Number Eight: Ask for help when you need it. Don't ever be scared of asking for help. Even if you can't say the words out loud you can message or sign or text or write to someone. It doesn't matter whether you need help with a big issue or a small one, reach out. This is really important if you feel that things are getting tough for you, or you are having thoughts about harming yourself or someone else. There are services out there in the community that can help. So don't struggle alone.

Number Nine: Find your Tribe. Many autistic people have felt lonely or isolated in their life and many talk about feeling that they don't fit in. The truth is, there are many people who feel like this, whether they are on the spectrum or not, and until we can learn to reach out to each other, things won't change. There may be some local autism support groups you can join or online forums. Or you might prefer to join a group that shares interests such as a walking group, book club, gaming convention group, astronomy fans, pub meet-ups ... the list is endless! Don't do it in a way which overwhelms you, take small steps to meet other people. You will be anxious the first time but it will get a little easier each time after that. You never know who you might meet and you may even become the inspiration for someone else to get an assessment or to be brave enough to cope with their own autism journey.

Number Ten: Don't ever give up. There will be days when it will all feel too much. Those days where it's hard to get out of bed or to function or to do anything at all. That's okay - but don't let every day be like that.

There's too much for the world to offer you. And the world needs you.

Ask for help if you need it. But don't ever give up.

Chapter 4

Resources

Thankfully, information available on autism has increased significantly over the last few years. There are many websites, research papers and organisations which produce extremely helpful resources. I am not affiliated to any of the following organisations/ authors but have simply found their resources to be extremely beneficial both for increasing my own knowledge and for sharing with the people I have worked with.

As previously mentioned, the National Autistic Society's website is comprehensive and has information on most subjects, including employment rights, reasonable adjustments, support in schools, welfare benefit information and signposting to support services regionally and nationally: *www.autism.org*

There are also other support groups, charities and organisations in your area whose details you can access through Google, by typing "Autism Support UK".

There are mental health services and support organisations that will be specific to your area. You can google this or contact your GP surgery or local authority office to ask for the details.

In an emergency you can search online for "Mental health crisis help" for your local service, or call 111. If you need emergency services, call the usual 999 number. The Samaritans are also available every day on 116 123. Please note, these telephone numbers are for services in the

United Kingdom only. For other countries you will need to check your own local emergency contacts and provisions.

Ambitious About Autism is a national charity that offers information, support and employment opportunities for people on the spectrum: ambitiousaboutautism.org.uk

Books

There are many books on autism, here are a few I would recommend:

"Neurotribes – The legacy of autism and how to think smarter about people who think differently" – Steve Silberman (Allen and Unwin, 2015)
Winner of the Samuel Johnson's Prize for non-fiction, Sunday Times and New York bestseller. The culmination of 15 years of work by an American investigative journalist, the book is an in-depth work on the social history of autism and challenges conventional thinking about it as a condition.

"The Autistic Brain" – Temple Grandin (Rider Press, 2014)
Temple Grandin is a well-known voice in the world of autism. She is an autistic adult, speaker and author of six books on the subject, with this book being the most well-known. Often used as a reference book for professionals, it is an in-depth technical science book and also refers to her own experiences on the spectrum.

"Fingers in The Sparkle Jar – A Memoir" – Chris Packham (Ebury Press, 2017)
A memoir of his life by the wildlife expert and TV presenter, which also led to a TV documentary, "Asperger's' and me". In the book he talks about his early years and it is written in a variety of first and third person styles as a narrative memoir.

"We're Not Broken – Changing the Autism Conversation" – Eric Garcia *(Houghton Mifflin, 2021)*
This American book is written by the assistant editor of *The Washington Post* who has a diagnosis of autism. The book focuses on the social and policy gaps that exist in the US for people on the spectrum, such as education and health care provision, with contributions from the autistic community.

"The Electricity of Every Living Thing – A Woman's Walk in the Wild to Find Her Way Home" – Katherine May *(Trapeze Press, 2019)*
A memoir of one woman's diagnosis of Asperger's' as an adult in 2016 and how she coped with this by walking in nature. Written by a published creative writer, the book is an inspirational re-telling of her walk along the South West Coast Path. It is similar in writing style to Raynor Winn's "The Salt Path" genre.

"The Complete Guide to Asperger's' Syndrome" – Tony Attwood *(Jessica Kingsley Press, 2008)*
A definitive classic textbook on Asperger's' Syndrome in adults and children written by an Australian Clinical Psychologist who has an expert clinical reputation in the field. A textbook genre, a resource for academics and professionals, the book includes case studies and quotes from people on the spectrum.

"The Reason I Jump – One Boy's Voice from the Silence of Autism" – *Naoki Higashida, translated by David Mitchell (Sceptre, 2014)*
A Number 1 *Sunday Times* bestseller (and subsequent award-winning TV documentary and film) that tells the story of a Japanese child with autism. Higashida wrote it at the age of thirteen and this and his other book, *"Fall Down Seven Times, Get Up Eight"* (*Sceptre, March 2018)* have been translated in the UK by David Mitchell.

"Explaining Humans – Winner of The Royal Society Science Book Prize 2020" – Camilla Pang *(Penguin, 2021)*
Written by an academic with a PhD in Biochemistry who was

diagnosed with autism as a child, described as an "exploration of human nature and the strangeness of social norms, written from the outside looking in". The book uses scientific principles to seek to explain why people behave socially in the ways that they do.

"Spectrum Women – Walking to The Beat of Autism" – Barb Cook and Dr Michelle Garnett (Jessica Kingsley, 2018)
This book is a compilation of 15 stories written by women on the autism spectrum with commentary by an Australian Psychologist. The women talk about their diagnosis of autism and how it impacts on their life and shows why autism in females is often misunderstood.

"Thriving with Autism – 90 activities to encourage your child's communication, engagement and play" – Katie Cook (Rockridge, 2020)

"Understanding and managing autism in children" – Harris (Independent, 2021)

If you enjoy watching talks on autism I recommend the series of TED Talks, which are available on YouTube.

There also a number of podcasts:

Autastic
What autism parents wish you knew
The Aspie World
Spectrum Autism Research
Sue Larkey Podcast
Neurodiverging
Parenting autism

Available on Audible, Apple, Google and other podcast apps.

Legacy

The story of this book started with the ending of another one.

I was working in an autism team developing new services and meeting amazing people. Amazing people with big, big stories.

In 2020 I had to leave that job. For my own well-being. The senior organisational culture changed and it became everything that it should not be. It broke my heart to leave but if I hadn't, it would have broken me.

As I prepared to say goodbye to my co-workers and to the autistic communities of people that I had met and walked alongside, it saddened me that their stories would remain unheard. That they sat inside them, and inside me.

And that's when this book was born.

I could not let those stories go unheard. I knew they were capable of changing the way that society sees and treats people who are "different" in some way.

I knew they were capable of changing the world. So, I asked for them. I asked people to bare their untold stories. And look how they did it. This book is the legacy of thirty years of work, of meeting over a thousand people, of a lifetime of trying to understand myself and the world around me, and of three years of writing, some of it during a worldwide pandemic. And this book?

This book is our legacy.

This book is for the new generations of autistic children who deserve acceptance and the opportunity to reach their potential in life.

This is for the adults missed as children, who have had to fight and struggle throughout their lives for understanding.

This is for the parents who have to fight every day to claw for support and understanding, who have to be in full warrior mode to get the help and acceptance that they and their families so desperately need.

This is for every teacher and doctor and nurse and police officer and social worker and therapist who doesn't know how to help but really wants to.

And this is for those people who went before, who had to bear their untold stories and never got the understanding and the belonging and the joy they so deserved.

Hear our stories.

Take them as our gift.

And now write your own.

<p align="center">~~~**~~~</p>

Acknowledgements and Thanks

My deepest gratitude and heartfelt thanks go to my tribe – the people behind these untold stories who gave their hearts, time and energy to this book. You know who you are. I could not possibly convey my thanks in mere words to you.

To the autistic communities and individuals whom I've been so privileged to know, work with and walk alongside. Hard battles won and lost at times, but we keep going in our efforts to change the world.

For the families and loved ones who fight every day. I see you.

For the wonderful colleagues and staff I have worked with, passionately striving to set up services and support people. Keep going, we need you guys more than ever.

To Rachel, Steph, Sue, Russ, Simon, G.C, David – thank you for everything, your friendship, passion and strength kept me going at times. And Steph – your comments, often inappropriate and far too rude to reprint here, have given me the laughs that I have desperately needed on dark days.

To the amazing author Beth Kempton – who helped me see that I am a writer, and gave me the belief, confidence and courage to sit and pull those words out from my head and heart into the world.

To my wonderful friend Ceri. How fortunate I am to have met you. And a shared autism story too.

In memory of DR – I'm sorry I was too late.

For JJ - who I met for all the right reasons. My friend, my anchor and father to a young lady who changes the world in her own beautiful ways. Keep on being you, Lara.

Huge thanks to AnnMarie, without whom this book may never have been born. Without your expertise, your knowledge and your beautiful heart, I would never have managed to get this far. Our shared book story has undoubtedly created a deep friendship during very difficult times for us both - thank you.

And to you – whoever you are and whatever your story is.

Thank you for being part of our story.

~~~***~~~

Ingram Content Group UK Ltd.
Milton Keynes UK
UKHW050659200623
423698UK00003BA/5

THE UNIVERSAL HOME DOCTOR

The Universal Home Doctor

SIMON ARMITAGE

faber and faber

First published in 2002
by Faber and Faber Limited
3 Queen Square London WC1N 3AU
Published in the United States by Faber and Faber, Inc.,
an affiliate of Farrar, Straus and Giroux LLC, New York

Photoset by Wilmaset Ltd, Wirral
Printed in Italy

A CIP record for this book
is available from the British Library

ISBN 0-571-215335

2 4 6 8 10 9 7 5 3 1

for Susan Elizabeth
and Emmeline Olivia

Acknowledgements

'The Shout' *Gravesiana, Aldeburgh Poetry Anthology*; 'The Twang', 'The English' *Times Literary Supplement*; 'The Laughing Stock' commissioned by BBC Ratio 4; 'Chainsaw verses the Pampas Grass', 'Assault on the Senses', 'A Nutshell', 'The White-Liners', 'Cactus', 'The Stone Beach' *Poetry Review*; 'The Keep' Marco Nereo Rotelli's *Bunker Poetico* project; 'The Nerve Conduction Studies', 'The Flags of the Nations' *reater*; 'Two Clocks' *Time's Tidings* (Anvil); 'Butterflies' commissioned by BBC (Poetry Proms); 'Incredible' *St Luke's Review* (US); 'The Golden Toddy', 'The Jay, The Hard' *London Review of Books*; 'The Night Watchman' *Atlanta Review* (US); 'A Visit' published to accompany Antony Gormley's *Poles Apart* exhibition, Jablonka Galerie, Koln; 'It Could Be You' *Sunday Times*; 'The Strid', 'Birthday' *PN Review*; 'Working From Home' *Heat* (Australia); 'An Expedition' *Rialto* (a version of 'An Expedition' was first performed in Goldthorpe's Yard as part of Wilson and Wilson's production of *House*); 'The Back Man', 'The Wood for the Trees', 'Salvador' *Arete*; 'Butterflies', 'The Laughing Stock' *Short Fuse Anthology* (US); 'The Summerhouse' *The New Republic* (US); 'All for One' *The New Delta Review* (US); 'The Strand' *The Yale Review* (US).

Contents

THE UNIVERSAL HOME DOCTOR

The Shout

We went out
into the school yard together, me and the boy
whose name and face

I don't remember. We were testing the range
of the human voice:
he had to shout for all he was worth,

I had to raise an arm
from across the divide to signal back
that the sound had carried.

He called from over the park – I lifted an arm.
Out of bounds,
he yelled from the end of the road,

from the foot of the hill,
from beyond the look-out post of Fretwell's Farm –
I lifted an arm.

He left town, went on to be twenty years dead
with a gunshot hole
in the roof of his mouth, in Western Australia.

Boy with the name and face I don't remember,
you can stop shouting now, I can still hear you.

The Short Way Home

Here's something you might want to consider.
If I suddenly hit the brakes at night,
for instance on the road between nowhere
and Scapegoat Hill, or on Saddleworth Moor,
I'm only going to reverse the car
thirty or forty yards, so the cat's eye
staring from the gutter might blink again,
taken in by the headlights on full beam.
You see, these things pop from their sockets
after so long, after so many wheels
hammering over, smashing their heads in.
Would you mind stepping out of the transport
and collecting it? Stay transparent, mind –
one hint of shadow and they vaporise.
Be see-through until you've made hand-contact.
And if you're worried about more traffic
coming steaming around this blind corner,
this accident black-spot where my father
once found a biker dead in his helmet,
then I'll punch that red, triangular switch
on the dashboard, trip the hazard-warning lights,
making the car radioactive with amber.
And once you're back in the passenger side
with the seat belt properly clunked and clicked
and I've geared up into fourth or fifth,
why don't you hand it over, the cat's eye,
thank you, which looks like a bullet in fact,
with no moving parts, just a metal case
and a blunt glass bead up front. Not much *use*,
unless you're the type who wants to sit there

with the curtains drawn, shining a torch
into its iris, looking for Jesus.
During my time, I've happened to notice
how the British Police Force handle a torch –
in the overarm, javelin position,
as do night-watchmen, maybe to option
bringing the rear end down like a truncheon
in one flowing movement, without backlift,
without harming the tender filament.
Bang – the weight of five two-volt batteries.
Whereas our grip on the same implement
would be underarm, as with a poker
or garden hose. Pistols are sometimes known
as side arms, right? I've never possessed one,
but as the years go by you lose the use
of your throwing arm to frozen shoulder,
and some old men can no more throw a ball
than they can levitate or somersault.

So there's the thing with the loose cats' eyes, yes.
True. But also the first snow of winter.
If I go downstairs to grind the coffee
and it's all white-on-white through the window,
the roads baffled with snow, nothing moving,
the great outdoors comatose and dreaming,
likely as not I'll open the front door
and scoop a handful from the windowsill.
You'll be half-asleep as I dollop it
on one of those weightless ice-cream wafers
made from communion bread and brown paper
then serve it upstairs like heaven on toast,
food a millionaire might get a taste for.
You'll throw back the sheets, open the curtains

and see that for once in my life, *I'm right*.
Don't ask me if you should eat the thing, though,
it was more of a concept. I can guess
the calorific value of fresh snow,
but it's those other toxins and poisons,
particulates arising from petrol fumes –
hardly the famous Full English Breakfast.
Let that melt and a pound to a penny
holy water won't be the consequence.
Days like those, I'd like to be motoring
through Christmas-card weather over the hills,
but that means an all-terrain vehicle
and snow-chains, which carve up the surface
and crunch all the pleasure out of the ride.
Better to hold back, wait for a full moon
and one of those planetarium nights,
then turn off the headlights and radio.
It's like driving on the pretty B-roads
above Camberwick Green after closedown.
The police wouldn't think much of it, mind,
they're not really that kind of animal,
not really driving-by-moonlight people,
but you might get away with a caution
by keeping a civil tongue in your head.
Be honest – they're not made from pig iron,
the cops, and no less human than we are
given the same uniform and pay-scale.

Does any of that appeal, or not? Don't
say yes just for the sake of saying yes,
I wouldn't want to get so far down the line
only to find you bored out of your box,
giving me one of those screen-saver looks,

or taking the side of the bed nearest
the fire-escape, planning a midnight flit.

But if that were the extent, if I went
so far each time but no further, could you
settle for as much? Could you live with it?

All for One

Why is it my mind won't leave me alone?
All day it sits on the arm of the chair
plucking grey hairs like thoughts out of my skull,
flicking my ear with a Duralon comb.

Evenings when I need to work, get things done;
nine o'clock, my mind stands with its coat on
in the hall. Sod it. We drive to the pub,
it drinks, so yours truly has to drive home.

I leave at sunrise in the four-wheel drive –
my mind rides shotgun on the running board,
taps on the window of my log-cabin,
wants to find people and go night-clubbing.

Social call – my mind has to tag along.
Hangs off at first, plays it cool, smiles its smile;
next minute – launches into song. Then what?
Only cops off with the belle of the belle

of the ball – that's all. Main man. Life and soul.
Makes hand-shadows on the living-room wall.
Recites *Albert and the Lion*, in French,
stood on its head drinking a yard of ale.

Next morning over paracetamol and toast
my mind weeps crocodile tears of remorse
onto the tablecloth. *Can't we be close?*
I look my mind square in the face and scream:

mind, find your own family and friends to love;
mind, open your own high-interest account;
offer yourself the exploding cigar;
put whoopee-cushions under your own arse.

It's a joke. I flounce out through the front door;
my mind in its slippers and dressing gown
runs to the garden and catches my sleeve,
says what it's said a hundred times before.

From a distance it must look a strange sight:
two men of identical shape, at odds
at first, then joined by an outstretched arm, one
leading the other back to his own home.

The Hard

Here on the Hard, you're welcome to pull up and stay.
There's a flat fee of a quid for parking all day.

And wandering over the dunes, who wouldn't die
for the view: an endless estate of beach, the sea

kept out of the bay by the dam-wall of the sky.
Notice the sign, with details of last year's high tides.

Walk on, drawn to the shipwreck, a mirage of masts
a mile or so out, seemingly true and intact

but scuttled to serve as a target, and fixed on
by eyeballs staring from bird-hides lining the coast.

The vast, weather-washed, cornerless state of our mind
begins on the Hard; the Crown lays claim to the shore

between low tide and dry land, the country of sand,
but the moon is law. Take what you came here to find.

Stranger, the ticket you bought for a pound stays locked
in the car, like a butterfly trapped under glass.

Stamped with the time, it tells us how taken you are,
how carried away by now, how deep and how far.

Chainsaw versus the Pampas Grass

It seemed an unlikely match. All winter unplugged,
grinding its teeth in a plastic sleeve, the chainsaw swung
nose-down from a hook in the darkroom
under the hatch in the floor. When offered the can
it knocked back a quarter-pint of engine oil
and juices ran from its joints and threads,
oozed across the guide-bar and the maker's name,
into the dry links.

From the summerhouse, still holding one last gulp
of last year's heat behind its double doors, and hung
with the weightless wreckage of wasps and flies,
moth-balled in spider's wool ...
from there, I trailed the day-glo orange power-line
the length of the lawn and the garden path,
fed it out like powder from a keg, then walked
back to the socket and flicked the switch, then walked again
and coupled the saw to the flex – clipped them together.
Then dropped the safety catch and gunned the trigger.

No gearing up or getting to speed, just an instant rage,
the rush of metal lashing out at air, connected to the main.
The chainsaw with its perfect disregard, its mood
to tangle with cloth, or jewellery, or hair.
The chainsaw with its bloody desire, its sweet tooth
for the flesh of the face and the bones underneath,
its grand plan to kick back against nail or knot
and rear up into the brain.
I let it flare, lifted it into the sun

and felt the hundred beats per second drumming in its heart,
and felt the drive-wheel gargle in its throat.

The pampas grass with its ludicrous feathers
and plumes. The pampas grass, taking the warmth and light
from cuttings and bulbs, sunning itself,
stealing the show with its footstools, cushions and tufts
and its twelve-foot spears.
This was the sledgehammer taken to crack the nut.
Probably all that was needed here was a good pull or shove
or a pitchfork to lever it out at its base.
Overkill. I touched the blur of the blade
against the nearmost tip of a reed – it didn't exist.
I dabbed at a stalk that swooned, docked a couple of heads,
dismissed the top third of its canes with a sideways sweep
at shoulder height – this was a game.
I lifted the fringe of undergrowth, carved at the trunk –
plant-juice spat from the pipes and tubes
and dust flew out as I ripped into pockets of dark, secret
    warmth.

To clear a space to work
I raked whatever was severed or felled or torn
towards the dead zone under the outhouse wall, to be fired.
Then cut and raked, cut and raked, till what was left
was a flat stump the size of a manhole cover or barrel lid
that wouldn't be dug with a spade or prized from the earth.
Wanting to finish things off I took up the saw
and drove it vertically downwards into the upper roots,
but the blade became choked with soil or fouled with weeds,
or what was sliced or split somehow closed and mended
    behind,
like cutting at water or air with a knife.

I poured barbecue fluid into the patch
and threw in a match – it flamed for a minute, smoked
for a minute more, and went out. I left it at that.

In the weeks that came new shoots like asparagus tips
sprang up from its nest and by June
it was riding high in its saddle, wearing a new crown.
Corn in Egypt. I looked on
from the upstairs window like the midday moon.

Back below stairs on its hook, the chainsaw seethed.
I left it a year, to work back through its man-made dreams,
to try to forget.
The seamless urge to persist was as far as it got.

The Strid

After tying the knot,
whatever possessed us to make for the Strid?

That crossing point
on the River Wharfe

which famously did
for the boy and his dog;

that tourist trap
where a catchment area comes to a head

in a bottleneck stream
above Bolton Abbey;

you in your dress of double cream,
me done up like a tailor's dummy.

Surely it's more of a lover's leap:
two back-to-back rocks

hydraulically split
by the incompressible sap of the spine;

let it be known
that between two bodies made one

there's more going on
than they'd have us believe.

Whatever possessed us, though?
Was it the pink champagne talking?

Or all for the sake of carrying on,
canoodling out of doors,

the fuck of the century under the stars?
Or the leather-soled shoes

with the man-made uppers,
bought on the never-never,

moulded and stitched
for the purpose of taking us

up and across, over the threshold
of water-cut rock and localised moss

in one giant stride,
bridegroom and bride?

A week goes by,
then the rain delivers:

you, like the death of a swan
in a bed of reeds,

me, like a fish gone wrong
a mile down river;

exhibits X and Y,
matching rings on swollen fingers,

and proof beyond doubt
of married life –

the coroner's voice, proclaiming us
dead to the world, husband and wife.

The Twang

Well it was St George's Day in New York.
They'd dyed the Hudson with cochineal and chalk.
Bulldogs were arse-to-mouth in Central Park.
Mid-town, balloons drifted up, red and white streamers

flowed like plasma and milk. The Mayor on a float on Fifth,
resplendent, sunlight detonating on his pearly suit.
The President followed, doing the Lambeth Walk.
It was an election year on both counts. In the Royal Oak

boiled beef was going for a song. Some Dubliner
played along, came out with cockney rhyming-slang,
told jokes against his own and spoke of cousins twice
  removed
from Islington, which made him one of us.

A paper dragon tripped down Lexington, its tongue
truly forked. Two hands thrust from its open throat:
in the left, a red rose; in the right, a collection box
for the National Trust. I mean the National Front.

The Laughing Stock

October. Post meridian. Seven o'clock. We've had tea.
Chip pans cool on pantry shelves. Now we can lounge
on broken settees, scoff bite-size portions of chocolate and
    fat,
crack open a tinnie or two. Skin up. Channel hop.

We're keeping an ounce of toot in a tin for a rainy day.
We talk about work – which corners we cut. Our dogs
lick at the plates on the floor, snort at the ashtray.
Our children are bored, they'll go in the army.

The news was the usual stuff. Like a fire
the telly stays on all the time and our faces and hands
are tanned with the glare. Sit-coms are *so* funny.
The nights draw in, like someone left a tap running.

We're watching a show: *How the Other Half Live*.
Apparently, even at this late hour of an evening, couples
are just setting out to eat. They're friends of the Queen,
as likely as not, and peasant cuisine is an absolute must,

with the wine of the month. Cutlery waits in position.
On FM stations, dinner-jazz plays through open curtains.

Arse-time. Weight off the spine. The hour of the couch.
Now and again, one of us scrubs up well, crosses
the border, gets so far then opens his cake-hole,
asks for meals by the wrong name, in the wrong order.

Why bother? The dishes can wait; we're washing our hair
in the sink, soaking our feet in a bowl. Our dogs
are a joke, disgusting, coming to sniff and to drink
like animal things at the watering hole.

The Strand

We were two-and-a-half thousand miles west
and still putting miles on the clock, driving
at night, the small wooden towns of the coast
coming up in the rain like cargo adrift
then falling away into dark. The road
followed the swell of the land, riding the waves,
then slowed in a town whose name I forget,
a place picked with a pin and an old map
by pricking the bent finger of Cape Cod.
This time we meant it. This time we'd drawn blood.

Evening darkness. Trespass. Walking blindfold
down a private road to a public beach
to fuck, like an order, lie down and fuck.
If the lighthouse shoots us one of its looks,

so what. Then back to the Anglified room
with its Lloyd-loom chairs, its iron bedstead
like the gasworks gates, its Armitage Shanks,
electric candles and motorised drapes.
We dug out the cork from a bottle of red
with the car key, drank from the neck, then slept
naked and drunk on the four-poster bed
with its woolsack mattress and stage-coach springs.
The fire – a paper-pulp, look-a-like log
in its own, flammable, touch-paper bag –
burnt down as neatly in the polished grate
as it should, made flames without smoke or ash
or heat, and got us to dream the endings

of afternoon films and old, hardback books.
A place like this could go up in a flash.

By day we looked for our octopus print
on the beach, but a high tide had been in
to clean and tidy the bay, to flush out
creases and seams. Houses of wood on stilts,
blasted by years and the flacking of salt,
stood back from the front, held on by their roots.
Rock pools were bleary with seaweed and brine.
We were writing our full names on the beach
with our bare feet when I stood on the bird.
Peeled from the sand, hauled and held by its bill,
its parasol wings swung open and out
in a sprained, unmendable twirl. Stone dead –
the sodden quills, the nerveless, leaden flesh.

This was the turning post, the furthest point.
Here was the archaeopteryx of guilt,
this dinosaur hatched from its fossil shell
to doodle-bug out of Atlantic skies
or strike home riding the push of the tide.
It had to be photographed, weighed and sized,
named and sexed, had to be hoisted and hung
by its sharp, arrowhead skull – like a kill.

Then what? Either I raised it to heaven,
arranged its bones as a constellation,
kept on running under the empty stars
of its eyes, under a snow of feathers.
Or I followed the fixed look on your face
to an unmarked circle of sand from where

we could double back, leave this gannet's corpse
beached between open water and blue sky,
eating into the beach, feeding the sea.

The Straight and Narrow

When the tall and bearded careers advisor
set up his stall and his slide-projector

something clicked. There on the silver screen,
like a photograph of the human soul,

the X-ray plate of the ten-year-old girl
who swallowed a toy. Shadows and shapes,

mercury-tinted lungs and a tin-foil heart,
alloy organs and tubes, but bottom left,

the caught-on-camera lightning strike
of the metal car: like a neon bone,

some classic roadster with an open top
and a man at the wheel in goggles and cap,

motoring on through deep, internal dark.
The clouds opened up; we were leaving the past,

drawn by a star that had risen inside us,
some as astronauts and some as taxi-drivers.

An Expedition

We started in over the Great Artex Shield,
ridge-walls taking the shine from the blades of the sleds,
the half-track finding it tough going indeed.
Permanence, ages thick, caked on to some depth.
All the tinned supplies found to be second rate
and the packet stuff got at by morning dew.
We pushed on through.

We lost time, as predicted, became bemused
in the Plains of Anaglypta, drifted for days in the rafts,
tied up each evening in a new swamp, achingly familiar.
Finally, using the paddles to dig, breaching the bank,
we poured through like blood from a blister.
All were rewarded with chocolate and spiced bread.
We pushed forward, ahead.

And the nights were so dark. A deep, concussive dark,
the sort that we carry ourselves, on the inside, under the skin.
And cold, so that bad dreams froze into rock-hard shapes
that wouldn't be thawed by light. And the noonday sun
was a twenty-watt bulb on a threadbare flex
giving watery shadows eighty or ninety feet long.
We dug in, pushed on.

And after the cold, the heat. We slept in the day,
moved at dusk, traversed the Bulkhead in the blackest hours,
bivouacked under a single star so the drop underneath
was too much void to be taken in. We crossed the Porcelain
    Rim
like soldier ants crossing an aeroplane wing, lost a horse

in the pyroclastic waste, overcome by fumes.
We pushed on through.

We sank a borehole through the plasterboard,
hacked away at what was underneath,
then wormed into potholes of wattle and daub,
shouted vast, echoing prayers into the cavity wall.
Here one of us performed the transillumination of a bird's egg
with a torch. More lonely than could possibly be true.
We pushed on through.

Here is the record of men lost:
two of dry-throat in the long yomp over Working Top;
one of leaded water at Stop Tap;
one who fell behind at Panhandle and never caught up;
one who slipped through a gap;
two of mirage madness in the clammy plains of Dolly Blue.
We pushed on through.

We swallowed our fear, descended the West Flue
by peristalsis almost, put down camp in cinders and soot.
Pemmican. Pabulum. The grub was handed out, communion
    performed
with toothpaste and a stick of chewing gum.
In the mantle, over the Hearth, hard evidence of early life –
spray art in an unknown alphabet. We sent word
tied to a pigeon's leg – it circled the bay,

fluttered back.
After that, we pushed on through. Elements now
without name or form. We put the last of the dogs to good use,
took notes, made maps, gave names, but for who?
For *whom*? Each heart went on. Where else to head for

but the fixed eventuality of earth, water and stone.
We pushed through for home.

The Stone Beach

A walk, not more than a mile
along the barricade of land
between the ocean and the grey lagoon.
Six of us, hand in hand,

connected by blood. Underfoot
a billion stones and pebbles –
new potatoes, mint imperials,
the eggs of birds –

each rock more infinitely formed
than anything we own.
Spoilt for choice – which one to throw,
which to pocket and take home.

The present tense, although
some angle of the sun, some slant of light
back-dates us thirty years.
Home-movie. Super 8.

Seaweed in ropes and rags.
The weightless, empty armour
of a crab. A jawbone, bleached
and blasted, manages a smile.

Long-shore-drift,
the ocean sorts and sifts,
giving with this, getting back
with the next.

A sailboat thinks itself
across the bay.
Susan, nursing a thought of her own
unthreads and threads

the middle button of her coat.
Disturbed,
a colony of nesting terns
makes one full circle of the world

then drops.
But the beach, full of itself,
each round of rock
no smaller than a bottle top,

no bigger than a nephew's fist.
One minute more, as Jonathan, three, autistic,
hypnotised by flight and fall,
picks one more shape

and under-arms the last wish of the day –
look, like a stone – into the next wave.

Salvador

He has come this far for the English to see,
arrived by bubble through a twelve-hour dream
of altitude sickness and relative speed, of leg room
and feet, headphone headache, reclining sleep.
Jet-lag slung from the eyes like hammocks at full stretch,
Meflaquin pellets riding shotgun in a blister-pack.
This far south for the English to see, as they say.
The hotel drives towards him up the street,
he turns the keyhole anti-clockwise with the key,
the water spins the plug-hole backwards as it drains.
He counts the track-marks in his upper arm
and those in the buttocks and those in the calves,
the pins and needles of shots and jabs, strains and strands,
spores going wild in the tunnels and tubes of veins,
mushrooming into the brain. A polio spider
abseils the drop from the sink to the bath.
Larium country – this far south to broaden the mind.
Look, learn, rise to the day, throw back the blind:
the blue-green flowers of the meningitis tree,
the two-note singing of the hepatitis bird,
the two-stroke buzz of the tetanus bee.
In a puff of chalk a yellow-fever moth
collides and detonates against the window frame.
Malaria witters and whines in the radio waves.
A warm, diphtherial breeze unsettles the pool.
Three hours behind and two days' growth –
hey you in the mirror, shaving in soap,
brushing your teeth in duty-free rum and mini-bar coke,
you with the look, you with the face – it's me, wake up.

The Wood for the Trees

It was the rainforest, so guess what, it pissed down.
And plant-life was the main point of view and not one

of the Leatherman's twenty blades could handle trust.
Trust in a twisted vine or knot in a tree trunk

as a short cut in bare feet back to a grass hut.
Trust in the gift of a green banana-leaf hat,

in the nous of the cockroach captain of a boat
through improbable land-locked dark, wheeling about

in an inch of slurry, seven days from the coast.
Trust in the line and the shining hook, that each cast

lands on the snout of a dogfish as it barks, sinks
to the lip of a catfish as it sleeps or sulks,

dazzles the rainbow bass draped in its national flag
of celestial globes on green-and-yellow flanks.

Trust in the fact that what we want least is to die.
In the neat symmetrical halves of night and day –

noon as a hob of heat to the crown of the head,
midnight's dark as a kettle of black tar set hard.

Trust in the light coming up as the light went down –
dusk as a campfire quashed with a flask of rain, dawn

as the dimmer-switch bloom of the filament plant.
In the upturned palm of a paddle as a plate,

trust in corn with the taste of gravel as enough,
in third-degree sunburn as a fact, in the myth

of the fish with a nose for the urinary tract
as myth, in the trance of a twelve-foot cayman, tricked

by the candle-bright beam of a four-inch torch.
In chicken bones thrown on bare earth as the true church.

In a thumb-print in blood as proof of a man's word,
the back of hand as a map of the known world.

At the furthest point away I woke one morning
after a night of shape-shifting and things moving

in the undergrowth like the wallpaper faces
of childhood, those monsters and other dark forces

alive in the bedroom curtains. Then I wondered
about home, the long journey backwards, and wandered

down to the stream for a drink. What followed the taste
was a sense of calm – calmness in its raw state

and a quietness almost internally near,
Then distant thoughts were suddenly blindingly clear.

The Golden Toddy

We hunted, swept the planet pole to pole
to capture a glimpse of that rare species.

Through a thermal lens we spotted the shoal,
picked up the trail of nuggety faeces

then tagged the shiniest beast in the pride,
mounted a camera on its gleaming horn,
bolted a microphone into its hide.
A first: toddies aflight, asleep, in spawn ...

After months in the field, the broken yolks
had gilded and glazed the presenter's boots;
the sponsor's lover wore a precious skull
for a brooch, out-glinting the best boy's tooth.

Rank bad form. But the creature itself shone,
perched on the clapper-board, the golden one.

Birthday

Bed. Sheets without sleep, and the first birds.
Dawn at the pace of a yacht.

The first bus, empty, carries its cargo of light
from the depot, like a block of ice.

Dawn when the mind looks out of its nest,
dawn with gold in its teeth.

In the street, a milk-float moves
by throw of a dice,

the mast to the east raises itself
to its full height. Elsewhere

someone's husband touches someone's wife.
One day older the planet weeps.

This is the room
where I found you one night,

bent double, poring over
the *Universal Home Doctor*,

that bible of death, atlas of ill-health:
hand-drawn, colour-coded diagrams of pain,

chromosomal abnormalities explained,
progesterone secretion,

cervical incompetence . . .
Susan, for God's sake.

I had to edge towards it,
close the cover with my bare foot.

Dawn when the mind looks out of its nest.
Dawn with gold in its teeth.

From the window I watch
Anubis, upright in black gloves

making a sweep of the earth
under the nameless tree,

pushing through shrubs,
checking the bin for bones or meat

then leaving with a backward glance, in his own time,
crossing the lawn and closing the gate.

The Flags of the Nations

The law requires that it is essential to use the correct coloured bag at all times.

White Nylon with
Orange Band:
ALL PATIENTS' PERSONAL SOILED
(dirty) CLOTHING.

White Nylon:
ALL SOILED (dirty) laundry and net
bags.

Clear Plastic:
Laundry FOULED with faecal matter,
blood, bile, vomit or pus. Fouled
items should be placed in a clear
plastic bag, and then into a white
nylon outer bag.

Clear Water-Soluble:
INFESTED (body lice and fleas).

Red Water-Soluble:
INFECTED laundry, if soiled, from
patients with or suspected of suffering
from Hepatitis A or B, Typhoid,
Paratyphoid, Salmonella, Shigella,
Cholera, Anthrax, Poliomyelitis,
Diphtheria & HIV.

All such infested/infected laundry
should be placed into the appropriate
water-soluble bag and then sealed in
an outer bag.

Green Plastic:
THEATRE linen only.

Yellow Plastic: Clinical waste for incineration.

Black Plastic: Non-infected household-type waste only. Papers. Flowers.

Splinter

Was it a fall in pressure or some upward force
that went to the head of that spikelet of glass
and drew it through flesh, caused it to show its face
so many years to the day after the great crash.

The Night-Watchman

Waking in cold sweat, he thought of the miller
dunking his head in his day's work
to guard against theft from his precious flour,
sealing every grain and ground in place
with the look in his eye and the twist of his mouth.

Even a finger, licked and dabbed for a taste
would leave a print, a trace. Then thought

of the deep-sea diver or astronaut, home at last,
who peeled the bedspread from his bed and caught
a strange impression in the cotton sheet,
a new expression buried in the pillow-case
beside his wife, and stood

a lifelong minute on the ocean-floor of outer space,
lead-limbed, ashen-faced.

A Visit

for AG

When I opened the door of the cage, the first had flown
from the rig of a pommel horse or the parallel bars
and had come to land on its feet, staking a claim
for a perfect score or a round of applause.
The second had walked the plank, or was poised
on the quivering lip of a diving board, ready to launch
and meet whatever elements might break its fall.
Across an empty room they aped each other, like for like,
and were cast as twins, but even to me it was plain enough
that one was a touching down to the other's taking off.
I paced out seven equal strides in leather boots
between the two, then killed some time in the gap,
the space which was also a force, a for and against
that kept them close and held them apart, and I sensed
a balancing act of sorts, a line to be crossed.
They were taller than me by as much as a hand,
and in sizing them up they followed suit, pressed back
against their metal frames to show off finer points:
the A-shape where the collar housed the neck,
the apple in the throat, like a clot, like an egg,
lips that were sealed with a smear of flux,
the seam – some International Date Line running crosswise
to the scalp, the cockpit of the frontal lobes,
the death-mask and the life-mask, facing up, exchanging looks.
True, side on they were ordinary men in the nude.
But fore and aft they lifted their wings to a height
that covered the join where solid earth meets open sky,
and one couldn't shield the world from the world's dark,
and one couldn't stoop or hunch to let in the light,

but they carried their weight, shoulder to wrist
with arms assumed into the leading edge of flight.
Thumped with a fist, they rang with a depth
of a church bell or cargo door slammed shut, and dust
was sunburnt skin, the orange-brown psoriasis of rust.
Within, one form held firm against the audience of air.
Without, one form encased the bubble of its heart.

In distant rooms came the circus of family and friends:
blotted faces leering out of picture frames; the man
who slept too long on his bed of nails, and turned
in the night, and rose at dawn in an aura of thorns,
pegs instead of body hairs, spikes which were thoughts.
And pipe-cleaner man with his igneous bones, pigeon-toed,
some cousin of the ploughshare and the tuning fork.

But the angels of iron, they were the things: flying machines
dreamed up, pilots and 'planes in the same breath.
Consider these works. Stand, dumb-struck in the field,
between the poles. Take in those forms: this earth-piece
bolted by its presence to a starting block;
this lectern, gliding by the metal pages of a book.

The Jay

I was pegging out your lime-green dress;
you were hoping the last of the sun
might sip the last few beads of drip-dry water
from its lime-green hem.

I had a blister-stigmata the size of an eye
in the palm of my hand
from twisting the point of a screw
into the meat of the house. Those days. Those times.

The baby bird was crossing the gravel path
in the style of a rowing boat crossing dry land.
Struck with terror when I held it tight
in the gardening gloves of humankind, we saw for ourselves

the mouse-fur face and black moustache,
the squab of breast-meat under its throat,
the buff-brown coat and blue lapels,
the painted inside of its mouth,

the raw, umbilical flute of its tongue
sucking hard at the sky for a taste of air.
Setting it free, it managed no more than a butterfly stroke
to the shade of an evergreen tree, where we let it be.

They say now that the basis of life
in the form of essential carbon deposits
could have fallen to earth as a meteorite, or comet,
and that lightning strikes from banks of static

delivered the spark that set life spinning.

But this three-letter bird was death, death thrown in from
  above,

death as a crash-brained, bone-smashed, cross-feathered
  bullet,

so we could neither kill it nor love it.

The Nerve Conduction Studies

We ask that watches and rings are removed.
We ask that trousers are rolled to the knees,
sleeves to the elbow. We ask for clean feet,
any wounds to be dressed, hands to be warmed

in the sink to bring blood close to the skin.
Would sir say sir was sensitive to pain?
Cold metal on bare flesh comes as a shock.
We loop conductive strips over the toes

and fingers, press conductive strips and pads
into the calves and wrists, and we ask
that electrolyte dripping from elbows
and heels not be mistaken for cold sweat.

We ask that questions of voltage are saved
till last; diabetics, for some reason,
feel less – we crank up the current, sometimes
forget, but in layman's terms we can state

that a small charge makes a tour of the nerves
by way of the brain. We measure the speed.
There, like the graph of the song of the whale
the trace comes up on the screen and we ask

for a second or third flick of the switch
if the jolt doesn't travel the distance
the first time. All in the head, is it not?
They say it's relative, but they don't say

to what. We ask that a pillow be placed
in the lap; we advise eyes to the front.
Humour is good – a good chance for a joke,
that it wouldn't take much to make sir talk

but a mind with nothing to hide or fight
is amazingly weak. In point of fact,
men with hard, dark faces are tickled pink.
Elderly women hardly even flinch.

We offer sweet tea in a plastic cup
and point to the door with a fountain pen.
Before starting up, unwind in the car:
let the sickness pass, let the windscreen clear.

Findings are by post except in the case
of freak results or a rare disorder.
These tests are well known to hold true; we trust
they prove nothing less than you dared hope for.

The White-Liners

They do the white line.
It's tough going, hard on the body, life on the road.
You find them everywhere: motorways, high streets, English
    country lanes.
They've done thousands of miles, leaving their trails behind.

They operate in traffic, sometimes at night.
Blind corners and accident black-spots are part of the job.
Their dreams are chevrons, zebras, pelicans and cats' eyes.
They eke out their stuff, cut it with all kinds of crud.

You'd think they could tell a few tales – you'd be wrong.
It's the classic case, the original one-track mind.
Years go by like cars, landscapes rise and fall
in front of their eyes, but the song is the same:

white lines, how they're the white-liners, doing the white line.

The Summerhouse

With the right tools it was less than a day's work.
It wasn't our trade, but a wire-brush was the thing
for fettling mould and moss from bevelled window frames.
Sandpaper took back old wood to its true grain.

Winter pressed its handshake, even through thick gloves.
From the boozy warmth of the boiler-room I lugged
a litre tin of Weatherseal, and popped the lid.
Strange brew. Varnish or paint? Water-based, it had a tone

or shade, but carried solvent on its breath
and held the stars and planets of a pinhole universe
suspended in its depth. Some gemstone in its liquid state –
it fumed when ruffled with a garden cane.

Winter stood on the toe-end of leather boots.
And as the substance in the tin went down it lost its shine
and from its lower reaches came a sluggishness –
a thick, begrudging treacle, and the colour brown.

Some change in temperature was the root cause.
Rifles stamped their feet and clapped their hands together
over on the firing-range. It was going dark
but unconcerned we dipped the brushes for a second coat.

It was time-travel, of a sort. Having given our all
to this chapel of sun-loungers and soft drinks,
to the obvious glory of ultraviolet light, we found ourselves
standing instead by a wooden shed, painted with mud and shit.

Butterflies

Is it astral alignment or plain old quirk of fate
that the road over the knoll takes a shot at the moon
or reaches out for the sun, like one of those phantom limbs
still alive and well in the minds of amputees?

Don't stop, there's nothing there. No marker stone,
no weather station locked in a white hut, no seat
for the view, no clockwork stereoscope with both eyes shut
and a slot for old money, jammed with a lolly stick.

Instead, just drive – it's a stepping off into the unknown.
Kids in the back of the car would sing out to take it at speed,
    release
the stomach's lepidoptera – red admiral and cabbage white –
like a million in used notes, swept up by a freak wind.

Even at our age and alone, some instinct in the toes or heel
wants to let rip over the brow of that hill, let body and soul
divide, the heart in its seat-belt, hands locked on the wheel
but the spirit propelled through the windscreen – weightless,
    thrown ...

True, people we know have gone up and never come down.
Timing is all it takes, some biker or driver at full pelt,
thinking the same thing, coming the other way. But in our
    world,
that's how these creatures form, how the wings are made.

The English

They are a gentleman farmer, living
on reduced means, a cricketer's widow
sowing a kitchen garden with sweet peas.
A lighthouse-keeper counting aeroplanes.

Old blackout curtains staunch the break of day.
Regard the way they dwell, the harking back:
how the women at home went soldiering on
with pillows for husbands, fingers for sons,

how man after man emerged at dawn
from his house, in his socks, then laced his boots
on the step, locked up, then steadied himself
to post a key back through the letterbox.

The afternoon naps, the quaint hours they keep.
But since you ask them, that is how they sleep.

It Could Be You

We interrupt our live coverage of the War
for details of tonight's National Lottery draw:

the winning numbers are fourteen, eighteen,
thirty-nine, forty-four, eighty-two, and ninety-one.

The bonus ball is number two-thousand-and-some.
A record jackpot pay-out will be shared between

winning ticket holders in Belfast, Aberdeen,
Milford Haven and East Acton. Now back to the action.

A Nutshell

It's too easy to mouth off, say
how this matchwood-and-cotton ship of the line
got where it is today,

how it put into port,
shouldered home through the narrow neck
of a seamless, polished-off ten-year-old malt,

came to be docked
in a fish-eye, bell-jar, wide-angle bottle
shipshape and Bristol fashion.

See, the whole thing was rigged
and righted itself at the tug of a string
or turn of a screw, main mast raised

to its full height,
every detail correctly gauged, taffrail
to figurehead, a model of form

and scale right down
to the glow of coal and the captain,
toasting himself in the great cabin.

It's the same kind of loose talk
that cost us dear, put fire in the chimney breast,
smoking the stork from its nest.

At the end of the day couldn't we meet
half-way, in an autumn field
in the stubble of hay,

hearing the chink, chink, chink
of cheers, prost, mud in your eye, and stumble
through gate or arch

to emerge on an apple orchard
in full cry, where tree after tree bends double
with glass, where every growth

blows a bubble or flask of fruit-in-the-bottle –
Jupiter, James Grieve, Ashmeads Kernel –
branch after branch of bottled fruit,

there for the picking, preserved in light?

Working from Home

When the tree-cutter came with his pint-size mate,
I sat in the house but couldn't think.
For an hour he lurked in the undergrowth,
trimming the lower limbs, exposing the trunks.

I moved upstairs but there he was, countersunk eyes
and as bald as a spoon, emergent in orange rays,
head popping out through leafage or fir,
a fairy light in the tree of heaven,

a marker-buoy in the new plantation of silver pine.
Or traversing, bough to bough, from one dead elm
to the next, or holding on by his legs only
or accrobranching the canopy. At lunch,

he pulled the wooden ladder up behind,
perched in the crown of a laurel, and smoked.
He nursed the petrol-driven chainsaw like a false arm.
The dwarf swept berries and beech-nuts into a cloth bag.

I was dodging between rooms now, hiding from view.
Down below they cranked up the chipping machine,
fed timber and brushwood into the hopper.
Through a gap in the curtains I looked, saw into its maw –

steel teeth crunching fishbone twigs,
chomping thick wood, gagging on lumber and stumps.
Sawdust rained into the caged truck.
Birds were flying into the arms of a scarecrow

on the Pole Moor, or leaving for Spain. I sat on the steps
between ground-floor and upstairs, thought of his face
at the bathroom window watching me shave,
his lips in the letterbox, wanting to speak.

Assault on the Senses

i) CATALOGUE

In the Line of Sight
mixed media:
carousel projection of assassinated world leaders viewed through telescopic sight consisting of spent bullet-casing and cross-hairs formed by two of artist's own eyelashes. Private collection.

What I Feel I Can't Touch, What I Touch I Can't Feel
mixed media/working model:
two coin-operated mechanical fun-fair 'cranes' in glass case, right claw wearing full-size boxing-glove, left claw wearing yellow washing-up glove, both suspended above one-hundred assorted family photographs belonging to artist, face up. One old penny per go. Private collection.

By Any Other Name
mixed media/working model:
cross-section of human head (nose-part moulded from artist's own sun-dried mucus) nasally exhaling carbon monoxide fumes generated by miniature petrol-driven engine housed within alabaster brain-cavity. Foregrounded by red rose wearing face-mask. Private collection.

Sweet Tooth
mixed media:
moulded impression of artist's own mouth, gums cast in boiled sugar, teeth sculpted from Kendal Mint Cake. Private collection.

Timing How Long I Can Stand a Loud Noise before Giving In
looped video presentation:
black-and-white film of artist in recording studio positioned
between two in-turned loud-speakers broadcasting increasing
volume of feedback. Foregrounded by graphic equaliser and
stopwatch. Private collection.

Walking on the Moon
colour photograph on teflon-coated aluminium:
self-portrait of artist's own toes painted as ten astronauts
with toe-nails as helmet visors, set against computer-
enhanced image of deep space. Private collection.

Music to the Ears
mixed media:
wall-mounted treble and bass clef fashioned from artist's
own ear-wax, vacuum-packed in transparent polythene.
Private collection.

Shit for Brains
mixed media:
glass case containing baked life-size brain sculpted in artist's
own excrement, positioned on domestic 'Libra' weighing
scales, overbalanced by tin of dog meat. Private collection.

Samson and Vagina
mixed media:
'Samsonite' model of female crotch contorted into facial
mask, wearing wig constructed from artist's own head of
hair grown to shoulder-length over several years. Private
collection.

Blood, Sweat and Tears
two framed pictures:
lettering and numbering of chemical equation for oil and chemical equation for canvas, painted in solution of artist's own blood, sweat and tears on tenterhooked rectangle of artist's epidermis. Private collection.

ii) REGISTER

The Gallery would like to recognise the inestimable contributions made by or on behalf of the following, without whom *Assault on the Senses* would not have been possible:

Gargantuan Interests Ltd
Raymond Kunt III
International Contaminates
Dr Malcolm Armsrace, OBE
The Gotten Family
Blabbermouth Promotions
The Gross Foundation
UltraBulk Foodstuffs
Sir Paul Oilfield
Mr Donald Tribeslayer, Jnr
The Capital Hospital for the Hopelessly Incurable plc

The Gallery also extends its acknowledgements to the great number of unlisted associates whose involvement gave shape and meaning to this exhibition.

Cactus

I'm putting all my hurt in one carrier-bag
and slinging the lot.
A sensitive tooth
that cowers from coffee and cold drinks;

a size-ten headache – drink-related – from last night,
worn like a crown
on the head of a child prince;
pins and needles, at it

like blackfly in the fingertips;
a shoulder-joint with metal fatigue;
stitch if I over-stretch or run;
grandmother's blessings peeling from both thumbs.

The barium meal of intense, personal hate.
Bad reviews for a good book –
dog turds on the lawn at first light.
My aching back.

The apostle spoon
of walking out and leaving a note;
the Maundy money
of things unsaid;

old photographs, dry bread.
The boomerang of a death
not happened, not yet.
That's about it.

Carting it down to the tip
I sense it coming together as one mass,
all its solids and slop
making a single, stubborn piece.

Splinters like wooden toothpicks
puncture the bag.
Peeling the plastic back I find
a cactus rooted in an iron pot –

rubbery flesh,
limbs like the limbs of a doll.
Its spikes stab the air
guarding sun-spot, jelly-tot buds

bearded with yellow fur.
So now I'm torn:
with its loveable form,
plausible fruits and cocktail sticks

it's a dangerous thing.
But tagged with its common name,
draped with a ribbon and sent to the right address,
actually it's a great gift.

Two Clocks

In the same bedroom we kept two small clocks,
one you could set your watch by, the other

you could not. The night we lost the good clock
under the bed the other seemed to know

to take its turn and was a metronome
until the lost clock was found. Then it stopped.

Like emergency lighting kicking in
during a power-cut, or biking it

half-asleep on the back of a tandem,
or gliding home with the engine broken.

And since neither of us can talk freely
on Albert Einstein's General Theory,

electromagnetic flux, black magic
or the paranormal, let us imagine

that all objects and events are open
to any meaning we choose to give them

and that if the absence of one timepiece
causes another to take up the pace

then these clocks could be said to demonstrate
some aspects of our love or private thoughts.

Stretching the point to another level,
maybe the effect is causal, and life –

if we could get things right on a small scale,
between people – might conform to this rule

of like for like; it could be that simple.
Maybe these clocks are a poor example.

The Back Man

Five strong, we were, not including the guide,
five of us walking a well-trodden path
through the reserve, from the camp to the stream
and the flooded forest on the far side.
Dragonflies motored past like fish on the wing.
Beetles lifted their solar-panelled shells.
A bird, invisible, ran through its scale
like a thumbnail strummed on a metal comb.
The branches of trees were shelves in a shop
selling insect brooches and snakeskin belts
and miniature frogs with enamelled heads.
The monkeys fancied themselves as soft toys.
Blue orchids offered themselves without shame.
Late afternoon, and the heat in the shade
was stale and gross, a queasy, airless warmth,
centuries old. I was the last in line,

the back man, when from out of nowhere
it broke, I mean flew at me from behind
and I saw in my mind's eye the carved mask
of its face, the famous robe of black fur,
the pins and amulets of claws and feet,
the crown and necklace of its jaws and teeth
all spearing into the nape of my neck.
I dropped the hunting knife and the shooting stick.

The rest of the group had moved on ahead.
The blades and feathers of grasses and ferns
conducted something in the air, but time
was static, jammed shut. Nerves strained with the sense

of a trap half-sprung, a pin almost pulled
and all noise was a tight thread stretched and thinned
to breaking point and blood in its circuit
awaited a pulse. The turnpike of a branch
bent slowly back to shape across the trail.
Up high, a treetop craned its weather vane;
a storm-cloud split and it started to rain.
I was shouldered home in the fibreglass tomb
of a yellow canoe. Then sat up straight –
alive. Unharmed, in fact. In fact untouched.

I've heard it said that a human face
shaved in the hairs on the back of a head
can stop a jaguar dead in its tracks,
the way a tattoo of Christ, crucified
across the shoulder blades and down the spine,
in past times, could save a thief from the lash.
Years on, nothing has changed. I'm still the man
to be hauled down, ripped apart, but a sharp
backward glance, as it were, is all it takes.
I sense it mostly in the day-to-day:
not handling some rare gem or art object
but flicking hot fat over a bubbling egg,
test-flying a stunt-kite from Blackstone Edge,
not swearing to tell the whole truth on oath
but bending to read the meter with a torch,
tonguing the seamless flux of a gold tooth,
not shaking the hands of serial killers
but dead-heading dogwood with secateurs,
eyeballing blue tits through binoculars,
not crossing the great ocean by pedalo
but moseying forward in the middle lane,
hanging wallpaper flush to the plumb-line,

not barrelling over sky-high waterfalls
but brass-rubbing the hallmarks of fob-watches,
lying on top of sex, in the afterwards,
not metal-detecting the beach for land-mines
but tilting the fins of pinball machines,
pencilling snidey comments in the margins,
not escaping into freedom or peacetime
but trousering readies extruded from cashpoints,
eating the thick air that blasts the escarpment,
not rising to the bait of a fur coat
but yacking on the cordless, cruising Ceefax,
checking the pollen-count and long-range forecast,
not whipping up the mother-of-all soufflés
but picking off clay pipes with an air-rifle
at the side-show, describing myself as
white in the tick-box, dipping the dipstick,
needling pips from half a pomegranate,
not cranking up the system to overload
but licking the Christian Aid envelope,
lining up a family photograph,
not chasing twisters across Oklahoma
but changing a flat tyre on the hard shoulder,
dousing for C4 with a coat hanger,
not carving a slice from the Golden Calf
but hiking the town's municipal golf course,
drowning an inner tube in a horse trough,
not feeling the sonic boom bodily
but swiping a key card in the hotel lobby,
easing up for the lollipop lady,
not inhabiting the divine sepulchre,
not crowing over Arctic adventure,
not standing gob-smacked beneath ancient sculpture,
not kneeling empty-handed, open-mouthed

at the altar, but in the barber's chair
or tattoo parlour, in a sleepy trance,
catching in the mirror the startled face
of some scissor-hand, some needle-finger.

The Keep

Sleep she on the eastern side,
holding a dream intact.

Sleep he turned to the west,
nursing a cracked rib.

Spine to spine, night over
turn they and face, make good

in the bed's trench. None break,
one keep in the bone crib.

Incredible

After the first phase, after the great fall
between floorboards into the room below,
the soft landing, then standing one-inch tall
within the high temple of table legs
or one-inch long inside a matchbox bed ...

And after the well-documented wars:
the tom-cat in its desert camouflage,
the spider in its chariot of limbs,
the sparrow in its single-seater plane ...

After that, a new dominion of scale.
The earthrise of a final, human smile.
The pure inconsequence of nakedness,
the obsolescence of flesh and bone.
Every atom ballooned. Those molecules
that rose as billiard balls went by as moons.
Neutrinos dawned and bloomed, each needle's eye
became the next cathedral door, flung wide.

So yardsticks, like pit-props, buckled and failed.

Lifetimes went past. With the critical mass
of hardly more than the thought of a thought
I kept on, headlong, to vanishing point.
I looked for an end, for some dimension
to hold hard and resist. But I still exist.